The Ultimate *Interactive* Basic Training Workbook

What You Must Know to Survive and Thrive in Today's Boot Camp

SB

Savas Beatie

New York and California

© 2007 by Michael C. Volkin

Cataloging-in-Publication Data is available from the Library of Congress.

First Savas Beatie edition 2007

ISBN 978-1-932714-32-6

SB

Published by
Savas Beatie LLC
521 Fifth Avenue, Suite 3400
New York, NY 10175
Phone: 610-853-9131

A licensed physician did not design the fitness program presented in this book. Consult a physician before starting any fitness program. All forms of exercise pose some inherent risks. The author, and everyone contributing to the publication of this book, advises readers to take full responsibility for their safety and know their limits. The statements and illustrations in this book are completely those of the authors and do not represent those of the United States military. See www.UltimateBasicTraining.com for more information.

All pictures taken in Iraq during Operation Enduring/Iraqi Freedom
Photographs by Jon Allen © 2004 fenix207@hotmail.com

Savas Beatie titles are available at special discounts for bulk purchases in the United States by corporations, institutions, and historical organizations. For more details, please contact us at Savas Beatie LLC, Special Sales, P.O. Box 4527, El Dorado Hills, CA 95762; e-mail us at sales@savasbeatie.com, or visit our website at www.savasbeatie.com for additional information.

The Ultimate *Interactive* Basic Training Workbook

Also by Michael C. Volkin

The Ultimate Basic Training Guidebook:
Tips, Tricks, and Tactics for Surviving Boot Camp

Just as I did in my former book *The Ultimate Basic Training Guidebook: Tips, Tricks and Tactics for Surviving Boot Camp*, this one is dedicated to the men and women of the U.S. military. They are the best soldiers the world has ever seen.

Thank you for your service and commitment to America and the world.

Table of Contents

Table of Contents (continued)

Part II: From Civilian to Military Fit: The Exercise Program

Photos and Illustrations

Figures

Tables

Photos and Illustrations (continued)

Preface

You are the future defender of our country, of our rights, and of the freedoms so many have fought so bravely for in past wars around the world. You are now about to embark on your military career, which begins with basic training. Drill Sergeants have only a few weeks to break down the civilian that you are and build you back up into an American soldier. Are you prepared, motivated, and determined to succeed? Basic training is a mental and physical challenge, but it can also be enjoyable and even fun. (Yes, you read that last sentence correctly.)

I designed this workbook as a supplement to my first book, *The Ultimate Basic Training Guidebook: Tips, Tricks and Tactics for Surviving Book Camp* (hereafter *Guidebook*). If you read both books carefully and apply the knowledge you will find inside <u>before</u> you arrive at boot camp, you will enjoy an insurmountable advantage during basic training. The odds are that you will have a much more enjoyable experience instead of a grueling, stressful one.

One of the best and most memorable days of your life will be the day you graduate basic training. The knowledge and concepts in these books will allow you to stand tall on <u>your</u> graduation day. You will wake up to a brighter sun on graduation morning. The air will smell fresher, your military uniform will fit like a glove, and you will feel like you are the most important person on the planet—because you will be. The multitude of unforgettable experiences you encountered during boot camp will coalesce into one ideal thought: I made it! I am a member of the smartest, toughest, most technologically advanced military that civilization has ever witnessed.

One soldier does make a difference.
One soldier can save lives.
One soldier can oppress tyranny.
One soldier can spread freedom and democracy.

You'll realize this and more on the day you stand tall with your fellow recruits at graduation. And on that day the books I worked hard to write for you will have meaning for both of us. I guarantee you I will feel as if I am right there standing with you. And in a sense, I will be.

Take a journey with me through these books and let me help guide you through basic training so you can achieve the maximum success in the easiest possible way. The rest is up to you.

I wish you good luck, because you will need it. If you read *The Ultimate Basic Training Guidebook* and finish the exercises in this workbook, you will need a lot less luck than the other recruits.

Introduction

I knew absolutely nothing about the military when I entered basic training. I had no immediate military family history and no prior desire to join any branch of the military. It was on the tragic morning of September 11, 2001, that I realized what I had been taking for granted all these many years. Freedom, as wonderful as it is, is an uphill struggle that comes with enormous responsibility. It wasn't so much a decision but a calling that yearned inside me after watching the enemies of Freedom and the Western way of life proclaim war against us. And so I joined the Army Reserves.

I departed for basic training without an ounce of military knowledge just one month after 9-11. However, I used this lack of knowledge to my advantage. I took notes on everything—everything. My goal was to record in some coherent way all the information I was learning so that no other recruit would have to go through basic training the same way—without any knowledge of what to expect or how to prepare for it.

I listened as hundreds of soldiers shared their advice, wisdom, and tips with me on surviving basic training. Shortly after basic training I was deployed to Iraq, where I served in Operation Enduring/Iraqi Freedom. Although I was very busy during my year in Iraq, I found some time to organize and flesh out my notes and assemble them into a practical basic training guidebook.

When I returned to the States I self-published my *Guidebook*. It sold out quickly. It was then I realized the true need for that book, and that I needed an experienced national publisher to reproduce it for a nationwide audience. Thankfully, I found one in Savas Beatie LLC, which redesigned and distributed it into the general book trade. I am proud to say that my *Guidebook* is now in its 7th printing and is a selection of the Military Book Club!

The Ultimate Interactive Basic Training Workbook is a natural follow-up to my *Guidebook*. Almost immediately after I published my first book, readers bombarded me with requests for more information, study guides—even test questions! Their requests made sense because the ability to test yourself will reinforce the information in both books. It creates an environment for new recruits to build on what they learned in the *Guidebook*. I think you will find *The Ultimate Interactive Basic Training Workbook* straightforward, jammed with information, and easy to understand and follow.

I encourage you to take advantage of the powerful fitness routine in this book. Scores of research hours and trial and error went into creating this program. It is designed specifically to get you ready for basic training. In my opinion, there is no other fitness program that will get you into shape faster for basic training.

It is important to understand that each branch of the military is different, but the core concepts to succeed at basic training are the same; and that is what this book teaches you. Therefore, just because I went through Army basic training does not mean this book does not apply to you if you are entering another branch of the service. This book (and my best-selling *Guidebook*) has been designed for you to succeed in <u>any</u> branch of the military you join.

As you begin your journey through my books and the United States military, never forget that success or failure now rests in your hands.

Graphics Key

Icons and Extended Answers

We have done everything we can to help make this workbook a rich and helpful primer that will help you prepare for basic training and your career in the military.

Throughout this book you will see a series of icons placed next to specific questions. You can click over to www.ultimatebasictraining.com/interactive and view interactive answers to the questions that have icons associated with them. Here are the icons you will see:

(video icon)

(audio icon)

(additional research / information)

(photo)

We hope you will avail yourself at every opportunity and take advantage of the *INTERACTIVE* aspects of this unique basic training workbook.

Chapter 1

Multiple Choice Questions

Below you will find a series of multiple choice questions specifically designed to build and test your knowledge of basic training. Circle the one correct answer for each question. The correct answers are listed in the back of the book, beginning on page 148.

1. What is a Drill Sergeant referring to when he tells you to fix your snake?

    A. The buttons on your uniform
    B. Your fly/zipper
    C. Your shoelace
    D. The sling on your weapon

2. What is the percentage of recruits who enter boot camp but don't make it through the first four years of their military service?

    A. 8%
    B. 12%
    C. 20%
    D. 40%

3. How many smoking breaks are allowed each day during basic training?

    A. 3
    B. 2
    C. 1
    D. 0

4. What is your Drill Sergeant referring to when she mentions a "hospital corner?"

    A. The medical center
    B. Your bed/bunk
    C. Your locker
    D. The area of the barracks where they put the "problem" recruits

5. The letter "R" in the phonetic alphabet stands for:

    A. Romeo
    B. Rifle
    C. Rotund
    D. Ralph

6. When eating meals during basic training, it is important to:

    A. Never eat your dessert before your meal
    B. Never eat dessert
    C. Never eat finger foods
    D. Make sure your napkin is tucked into your shirt before you eat the lobster

7. You can wear contact lenses during basic training:

    A. Anytime
    B. Only on days when you are not exposed to chemical training
    C. Upon approval of your Drill Sergeant
    D. Never

8. What is a TA-50?

A. A military issued flame thrower
B. A series of field equipment inspected often by Drill Sergeants
C. The final military exercise you must complete before graduating
D. A made-up term meant to trick me into picking a fictitious answer

9. After sneezing in formation while at the position of attention, it is important to shout:

A. "Recruit requests to be forgiven for unsoldierly conduct, Drill Sergeant!"
B. "Recruit is not worthy, Drill Sergeant!"
C. "Recruit requests a tissue, Drill Sergeant!"
D. Never sneeze in formation

10. What does MRE stand for?

A. Meals Ready to Excrete
B. Meals, Ready-to-Eat
C. Meals Required to Eat
D. Materials Resembling Edibles

11. What is the shelf life of a typical MRE stored at a constant 70 degrees Fahrenheit?

A. 2 months
B. 15 months
C. 50 months
D. 100 months

12. What is the name of the bread in MREs that is considered a revolutionary invention because of its ability to stay fresh for long periods of time?

    A. Wonder bread
    B. Pouch bread
    C. Endure bread
    D. Soft-chew bread

13. What item is found inside every MRE?

    A.   Ketchup
    B.   Mustard
    C.   Hot sauce
    D.   Rice

14. When did MREs replace C-rations?

    A. 1960s
    B. 1970s
    C. 1980s
    D. 1990s

15. Each MRE meal contains approximately how many calories?

    A. 600
    B. 800
    C. 1,000
    D. 1,200

16. MREs must be capable of withstanding parachute drops from:

    A. 150 feet
    B. 850 feet
    C. 1,250 feet
    D. 1,550 feet

17. How much does a single MRE cost your country?

    A. $1.25
    B. $3.25
    C. $5.25
    D. $7.25

18. A Drill Sergeant's hat is called a _____ hat.

    A. Campaign
    B. Caveat
    C. Kevlar
    D. Boot

19. Your Drill Sergeant tells you to pick up an AT-4. What is he talking about?

    A. An anti-terrorism manual
    B. A commonly used part found in a HUMVEE
    C. An anti-tank missile
    D. An army toothbrush especially designed to be packed in a soldier's
        rucksack

20. Just before firing an AT-4, what should a soldier yell to make sure the weapon does not affect nearby soldiers?

    A. Stand ready!
    B. Back-blast area all clear!
    C. Fire in the hole!
    D. Hey everyone, check this out!

21. When preparing a fighting position, camouflage may be necessary. If live foliage is needed, where should it be gathered from?

    A. As close to your fighting position as possible
    B. Anywhere, as long as there is a decent mixture of mud and foliage
    C. From as far as possible behind your fighting position
    D. From exactly 90 degrees from your current position

22. What is the Department of Defense's (DOD) health care program called?

A. DOD care
B. Simple care
C. Soldier care
D. TRICARE

23. How would you write the date April 2, 2006, in the format of the military dating system?

A. 02 Apr. 06
B. Apr. 02, 06
C. 06 Apr. 02
D. The second of April, 2006

24. If it is 2:00 a.m. and your Drill Sergeant asks you what time it is, how should you respond?

A. "O two hundred hours, Drill Sergeant!"
B. "Two hundred and zero hours, Drill Sergeant!"
C. "O hours and two, Drill Sergeant!"
D. "Drill Sergeant, you have been on my butt all day, let me sleep!"

25. Singing while marching in the military is called what?

A. Alto belting
B. A cadence
C. Octave marching
D. Singing while marching

26. The standard military-issue weapon is a:

A. M16/A2
B. M16/A4
C. M61/A2
D. M61/A4

27. Which of the following is not one of the four fundamentals of marksmanship?

    A. Steady Position
    B. Proper Aim
    C. Breathing
    D. Index locking

28. Without investigating the cause of a stoppage or jam on your rifle, a recruit should apply what to try and rectify the problem?

    A. Vaseline
    B. SPORTS
    C. The firing pin
    D. A Drill Sergeant

29. What is the weight of a standard M16/A2 rifle without a magazine or sling?

    A. 3.92 pounds
    B. 5.51 pounds
    C. 7.78 pounds
    D. 9.44 pounds

30. What is the maximum range of an M16/A2 rifle?

    A. 800 meters
    B. 3,600 meters
    C. 4,100 meters
    D. 6,200 meters

31. What is the basic ammunition load in a magazine for the M16/A2 rifle?

    A. 10 rounds
    B. 20 rounds
    C. 30 rounds
    D. 40 rounds

32. What is the length of a standard M16/A2 rifle?

    A. 33 5/8 inches
    B. 34 5/8 inches
    C. 37 5/8 inches
    D. 39 5/8 inches

33. Which of the following is true:

    A. Take all criticism from a Drill Sergeant personally
    B. Always try to stand out and be a leader when around Drill Sergeants
    C. You should always try to make friends with your Drill Sergeant
    D. You should never try to make friends with your Drill Sergeant

34. In what year was the Geneva Convention regarding the treatment of civilians signed?

    A. 1947
    B. 1949
    C. 1952
    D. 1965

35. As a POW, what is the only information you are required to provide your captors?

    A. Name
    B. Age
    C. Rank
    D. All of the above

36. When is the recipient of a Medal of Honor entitled to a salute?

    A. Only if the recipient is an officer
    B. Only if the recipient is enlisted (i.e., Sergeant)
    C. Whether the recipient is an officer or an enlisted man/woman
    D. Never

37. How often should a challenge and password be changed?

A. Every hour
B. Every six hours
C. Every 24 hours
D. Never

38. Which branch of service is known for turning a small budget into firepower?

A. Army
B. Air Force
C. Marines
D. Navy

39. Which branch of service nicknames its soldiers "Jarheads?"

A. Army
B. Air Force
C. Marines
D. Coast Guard

40. To gain respect from a Drill Sergeant, you should do all of the following except:

A. Speak softly
B. Be attentive
C. Be confident
D. Be loud

41. Which of the following sentences most accurately portrays basic training?

A. Basic training is 5% mental and 95% physical
B. Basic training is 25% mental and 75% physical
C. Basic training is 75% mental and 25% physical
D. Basic training is 95% mental and 5% physical

42. What is the main goal of a Drill Sergeant?

  A. To intimidate and train a recruit
  B. To criticize a recruit
  C. To break a recruit down as a civilian and build a recruit up into a soldier
  D. To motivate a recruit

43. What is the best way to approach your fellow recruits when you first arrive at basic training?

  A. With small talk
  B. Offer to help shine their boots
  C. Do not approach your fellow recruits; allow them to approach you
  D. Let them know you had a relative who has been through basic training before

44. If a Drill Sergeant asks why you joined the military, you should respond by saying:

  A. I need a job
  B. I love my country
  C. I joined for the college money
  D. My parents made me

45. When preparing for basic training, it is best to perform your workout routine during the:

  A. Early morning
  B. Late morning
  C. Early evening
  D. Late evening

46. Why should a recruit go to bed at 4:30 p.m. when preparing for basic training?

    A. To catch up on sleep before you arrive for basic training
    B. To anticipate jet lag
    C. To avoid eating a dessert after dinner
    D. To avoid getting tempted to party with your friends

47. When preparing for basic training:

    A. Limit your snacks to potato chips and non-chocolate items
    B. Limit your snacks to chocolate items only
    C. Don't snack in the evening
    D. Don't snack at any time, period.

48. How many square meals are you provided each day during basic training?

    A. One
    B. Four
    C. Two
    D. Three

49. What is a Drill Sergeant referring to when he talks about a "pass?"

    A. The right to proceed to the front of the chow line
    B. Your ability to graduate early due to a civilian skill you possess
    C. A permit to enter or leave a military installation for a given period of time
    D. A special card you can use at your discretion which will prevent a Drill Sergeant from yelling at you for 24 hours

50. What type of luggage should you avoid bringing to basic training?

    A. Single-color luggage
    B. Designer luggage
    C. Luggage with zippers
    D. Luggage with buttons

51. Your most memorable day at basic training will most likely be:

    A. Your first day
    B. The first time you interact with a Drill Sergeant
    C. Graduation day
    D. The first time you fire your weapon

52. When choosing your meals at basic training, it is important to always choose the following side dish if it is an option:

    A. Potatoes
    B. Rice
    C. Cranberry sauce
    D. Bread

53. The fastest way to eat your meals at basic training is:

    A. Tilt your head back and shove forkfuls of food down your throat
    B. Dilute everything in water, then drink the water
    C. Put all your food together in a bowl
    D. Make a sandwich out of everything

54. Eating desserts at basic training will:

    A. Get you in trouble
    B. Fill your stomach with empty calories
    C. Take time away from filling your stomach with protein
    D. All of the above

55. Which of the below should you add the most to your food?

    A. Ketchup
    B. Salt
    C. Pepper
    D. None of the above

56. If a Drill Sergeant tells you to be in formation in 45 seconds, you should be there in:

    A. 15 seconds
    B. 45 seconds
    C. One minute
    D. Whenever you feel like it

57. Your military boots come equipped with what are called:

    A. Arch supporters
    B. Flat jack tongues
    C. Quick tie laces
    D. Shock-absorbing soles

58. A _____ is a corner of a made-up bunk in which the sheets have been neatly and securely folded.

    A. 45-degree corner
    B. Hospital corner
    C. Edge perfect corner
    D. Quarter tight corner

59. How do you say the letters HJ in the phonetic alphabet?

    A. Horse Juniper
    B. Horse Juliet
    C. Hotel Juniper
    D. Hotel Juliet

60. What is the best way to handle your financial matters before you leave for basic training?

    A. Leave blank checks at home so someone can pay your bills
    B. Assign someone you trust general power of attorney
    C. Assign someone you trust specific power of attorney
    D. All of the above

61. How many suitcases should you pack when leaving for basic training?

    A. One
    B. Two
    C. Three
    D. Four

62. Which of the following is the least important to pack for basic training?

    A. Stamps
    B. Long distance calling cards
    C. Stationery
    D. Non-prescription drugs

63. Regarding prescription drugs at basic training:

    A. You can use them only if you show symptoms
    B. You can not use them for any reason
    C. They are only allowed with a doctor's note
    D. You can use them only if you share with others

64. You can remove snack-related food from the chow hall:

    A. Only on snack days
    B. Only on weekends
    C. Only on Sundays
    D. Never

65. Showing your palm while you salute signifies:

    A. Respect
    B. Great form
    C. You are giving up
    D. You are saluting a female officer

66. At basic training, you should put your initials on:

    A. Nothing, because nothing belongs to you
    B. Only your clothing
    C. Other soldiers' belongings
    D. All of your items

67. Which is true regarding phone cards during basic training?

    A. You can not use them
    B. Make sure they match your uniform
    C. Buy ones where the pre-recorded message doesn't talk too much
    D. Be sure to have an extraordinary amount of minutes on them

68. Which is true regarding razors at basic training (for males)?

    A. Never get caught with one in your pocket
    B. Carry one only if you forgot to shave
    C. Carry one in the evening in case you get a five-o'clock shadow
    D. Always carry one in your pocket

69. Regarding hair cuts for females:

    A. Wait until you get to basic training to have it cut
    B. Get it cut by a professional before you leave for basic training
    C. If you have a note from your stylist, the military will not touch it
    D. If you get it shaved as short as a male's, you might be required to
    live in male barracks

70. Drill Sergeants are allowed to hit you:

    A. Anytime they want
    B. Anytime you upset them
    C. Only when the senior Drill Sergeant is around
    D. Never

71. What is the meaning of "HUA," or "hooah?"

    A. I hear you, I understand you, and I acknowledge your statement
    B. Refers to, or means, anything other than "no"
    C. An all purpose expression
    D. Any or all of the above

72. About what percentage of recruits fail basic training?

    A. 1-5%
    B. 10-15%
    C. 20-25%
    D. More than 25%

73. If you decide you don't like basic training when you arrive:

    A. You can tell your Drill Sergeant and s/he might be able to get you honorably discharged
    B. You can return home at any time
    C. You can transfer to the Peace Corps with no questions asked
    D. It is extremely difficult to get honorably discharged

74. How far is a "klick" in the military?

    A. Approximately 1/2 mile
    B. Approximately 1 mile
    C. Approximately 1 ½ miles
    D. Approximately 2 miles

75. The term "leave" in the military refers to:

    A. A day in basic training when no exercises occur (usually a Sunday)
    B. Vacation, or "liberty"
    C. The right to go to the bathroom without asking permission
    D. Graduation day at basic training

76. Fireguard refers to:

A. A kitchen appliance you use when preparing meals
B. A duty (often at night) that requires a recruit take head count, guard other soldiers, and perform chores upon the Drill Sergeant's discretion
C. A piece of chemical equipment you will be issued at basic training
D. A recruit who keeps an eye out for Drill Sergeants while other recruits try to sneak cigarettes

77. If your Drill Sergeant assigns you to KP, you can expect a day:

A. In the field
B. In the kitchen
C. On guard duty
D. In bed

78. The UCMJ refers to:

A. The standard rules to wearing a military uniform
B. A set of codes used to get on and off military bases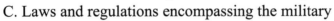
C. Laws and regulations encompassing the military
D. Your personal files to which your Drill Sergeants will have access

79. What phrase do Army Drill Sergeants have on their badges?

A. "Like no other"
B. "We are mean and proud of it"
C. "Training to perfection"
D. "This we'll defend"

80. ASVAB is a nickname Drill Sergeants have for what?

A. A symptom most recruits get upon arriving ar basic training
B. A military test
C. A piece of field equipment used to dig fighting positions
D. Recruits who miss their mommies

81. A recruit should always expect to _____ at basic training.

    A. Get a day off every now and then
    B. Lose weight
    C. Make friends
    D. Get sick

82. Which branch has what most consider to be the most difficult basic training program?

    A. Navy
    B. Air Force
    C. Army
    D. Marines

83. What do female recruits do during their "time of the month?"

    A. Nothing different
    B. Take temporary time off
    C. Tell their Drill Sergeant
    D. Have special access to bathroom breaks

84. What type of liquid is used to heat the food in an MRE?

    A. Mercury
    B. Saline solution
    C. Water
    D. Cooking oil

85. When a Drill Sergeant says you are going to get "smoked," what does that mean?

    A. A Drill Sergeant is going to wake you up in the middle of the night
    B. You will have to do an intense physical workout as punishment for an infraction
    C. You will have to restart basic training from day one
    D. You will have to lead the formation

86. Which of the following should you always do at basic training?

    A. Secure your wall locker
    B. Volunteer
    C. Brush your teeth before and after training
    D. All of the above

87. An Article 15 is:

    A. A paper in your file that contains all of your medical records
    B. A rock band who will be performing at your graduation
    C. A newsletter for recruits issued during basic training
    D. A section of the UCMJ that provides for swift non-judicial punishment for minor offenses

88. About what percentage of all jobs in the military are non-combat occupations?

    A. 10
    B. 25
    C. 50
    D. More than 75

89. In the marching movement *left face*, the command *left* is known as the:

    A. Command of execution
    B. Turning command
    C. Preparatory command
    D. Preposition command

90. In the marching movement *left face*, the command *face* is known as the:

    A. Command of execution
    B. Turning command
    C. Preparatory command
    D. Preposition command

91. What are the Geneva Conventions?

    A. Treaties designed for the planning of rescue missions
    B. Treaties designed for the treatment of terrorists
    C. Treaties designed that set the standard for American law for humanitarian aid
    D. Treaties that set the standards for international law for humanitarian concerns

92. Where were the Geneva Conventions written?

    A. New York, United States
    B. Geneva, Brazil
    C. Geneva, Switzerland
    D. The Hague, Belgium

93. What is "inflection" as it relates to the military?

    A. A term used when a male recruit has to bunk with a female recruit due to lack of room
    B. What happens to a wound when it is not properly covered
    C. The varying pitch of the voice of an individual giving commands
    D. A series of shots you receive before departing for boot camp

94. What command revokes a preparatory command?

    A. "As you were!"
    B. "Revoke!"
    C. "Command rescinded!"
    D. "Forget about what I said!"

95. What does the color white represent in the American flag?

    A. Honor for vigilance
    B. Purity and innocence
    C. Perseverance
    D. Justice

96. What is a guidon?

    A. A piece of equipment that attaches to your canteen
    B. A marching command that rescinds the last command given
    C. A soldier known as the clown of the bunch
    D. A company, battery, or troop identification flag

97. Who carries the first-aid pack in combat?

    A. The commander
    B. Every sergeant
    C. Every private
    D. Every soldier

98. Which of the following methods should not be used to clear an obstruction from the throat of a conscious victim?

    A. Back blows
    B. Abdominal thrusts
    C. CPR
    D. Chest thrusts

99. Which of the following is not a type of fracture?

    A. Open
    B. Bone
    C. Compound
    D. Simple

100. What does the color black represent on a military map?

    A. Vegetation
    B. Relief features and elevation
    C. Man-made objects
    D. Populated areas

101. Which of the following is not a type of "north" on a military map?

    A. High
    B. Magnetic
    C. True
    D. Grid

102. What is the United States' policy on the use of biological weapons in a conflict?

    A. We will use them first, if necessary
    B. We will never use them
    C. We will use only after the enemy uses them
    D. We will use them at our discretion

103. What can not be used to camouflage shiny areas on equipment?

    A. Earth
    B. Sand
    C. Paper
    D. Clay

104. What is a rally point?

    A. An area for soldiers to gather for motivational purposes
    B. A piece of equipment used to sharpen the tip of a bayonet
    C. An area where soldiers convene after it has become dispersed
    D. A nickname for the fourth week of basic training

105. What does the military recognize as the most important need in a survival situation?

    A. MREs
    B. Matches
    C. Water
    D. Blankets

106. Where would you most likely find a BDU or ACU?

    A. In your paperwork
    B. On a flagpole
    C. On a soldier's body
    D. In your recruiter's office

107. Which of the following is often referred to as the "backbone" of the military?

    A. The commander-in-chief
    B. Officers
    C. Privates
    D. Sergeants

108. You will not receive any mail at basic training until:

    A. Your recruiter finalizes your paperwork
    B. You complete all your medical testing
    C. You get to basic training
    D. Your third week of basic training

109. Drill Sergeants have to _____ to become a Drill Sergeant.

    A. Be active duty military personnel
    B. Take a class on how to make recruits feel bad
    C. Pass a rigorous and stressful course
    D. Sign up on a list that sometimes has a two-year waiting period

110. Why is basic training sometimes referred to as "boot camp?"

    A. Because many people fail, and a Drill Sergeant gets to give a recruit "the boot"
    B. This is where a recruit is first issued combat boots
    C. In the past, new recruits were called "boots"
    D. Because recruits spend most of their time in combat boots

111. What is the term/nickname Drill Sergeants give recruits who have to start basic training all over again?

    A. Long haulers
    B. Recycled
    C. Born agains
    D. Square one'rs

112. What is the meaning of a salute?

    A. To greet with an expression of welcome or respect
    B. To give affirmation
    C. To show support
    D. To acknowledge rank

113. When standing at the position of attention, your feet should be _____ degrees apart.

    A. 25
    B. 45
    C. 90
    D. 180

114. Which branch of service requires you to do pull ups to pass a fitness test?

    A. Army
    B. Navy
    C. Marines
    D. Air Force

Chapter 2

True or False

The following statements are either true or false. Circle the correct answer and then look up your response in the back of the book. The answers begin on page 165.

1. Direct deposit is mandatory for military pay at basic training. T/F

2. Your battle buddy will most likely be the same age and race as you. T/F

3. If a Drill Sergeant smiles at you, it is important that you smile back as soon as possible. T/F

4. Before you leave for basic training, it is important to know the arch type of your foot. T/F

5. When stretching your quadriceps muscle, you should put your leg behind your back and pull your toe toward the sky. T/F

6. A stride is calculated by measuring the distance of ten normal sized steps and dividing the distance you walked by ten. T/F

7. If you have a proper running movement, your heel should touch the ground first. T/F

8. Your foot should land under your body when you are running. T/F

9. If you are a male, it is a good idea to shave your head before you get to basic training. T/F

10. Using the machines in the gym to prepare my muscles for basic training is a great idea. T/F

11. There is no mail at basic training. T/F

12. An Article 15 is a section of the UCMJ that provides for swift non-judicial punishment for minor offenses. T/F

13. Cell phones are allowed at basic training. T/F

14. Women comprise approximately ten percent of the total population of the U.S. Military. T/F

15. Your Drill Sergeants will allow you to use an electric razor at basic training. T/F

16. Drill Sergeants will only let you bring one type of cologne or perfume with you to basic training. T/F

17. Female Drill Sergeants are usually a lot nicer than male Drill Sergeants, so if you have to ask for a favor, ask a female Drill Sergeant. T/F

18. Sick call is a great way to get out of daily drill and spend a relaxing day getting medical attention. T/F

19. Be sure to run with your buttocks slightly sticking out. Although this will feel uncomfortable, it will streamline your running movement. T/F

20. Do not bounce when you run, it wastes energy. T/F

21. When running, be sure to maximize your movement by pushing off with your toes. T/F

22. Basic training is very different depending on which military base you get assigned to attend. T/F

23. When celebrating your birthday at basic training, it would probably be best to keep it to yourself. T/F

24. Working out before breakfast allows your body to use stored fat as fuel, instead of carbohydrates. Thus, you burn more fat by working out before breakfast as opposed to after breakfast. T/F

25. Drill Sergeants are former soldiers who are not currently enrolled in the military. T/F

26. Each physical training session at basic training is comprised of three parts: warm-up, conditioning, and cool down. T/F

27. Recruits are soldiers who have not yet graduated basic training. T/F

28. The words rifle and gun are interchangeable in the military. T/F

29. A Swiss Army Knife is very handy to have at basic training. T/F

30. Never lean on anything in basic training. T/F

31. During basic training, you can only drink alcohol once a month, more than that will get you in trouble. T/F

32. A Drill Sergeant's job is to train recruits to work as individuals. T/F

33. When in class, keep your back straight and appear attentive. T/F

34. Showing your own style of a salute is a great way to impress your Drill Sergeant. T/F

35. A warrant officer is a military officer with a misdemeanor or felony on his/her record. T/F

36. Graduating from military basic training looks great on a resume. T/F

37. Day 1 in basic training is often the easiest. This is the only day where you can relax and be with new friends. T/F

38. If you get tired during a run with your soldiers, try walking to save your strength, then play catch up later. T/F

39. Becoming religious is a good idea at basic training. T/F

40. You can't call yourself a veteran unless you kill someone during a wartime operation. T/F

41. Rubbing your eyes after experiencing the gas chamber is a great way to ease any discomfort you are feeling. T/F

42. There is no need to salt and pepper your food when eating, the military chefs do this for you. T/F

Chapter 3

What Would You Do?

Below are a series of questions regarding a host of issues you might encounter during basic training. Do you know what you would do if any of these situations arise? Answer each question as fully as you are able. Remember, telling the answer to yourself is only half the battle. Writing it out will help you think it through, and help you remember it.

1. You are in class learning about the Uniform Code of Military Justice (UCMJ). The weather is snowy and the temperature is below freezing. You have been in class for hours and the classroom is dark because of an ongoing slide presentation. The Drill Sergeants gave strict orders not to talk to any recruit for any reason. The heat in the room is toasty warm, and you notice the recruit to your left nodding off to sleep. You know if that recruit falls asleep and is caught by a Drill Sergeant, everyone in the room will be doing exercises. What, if anything, do you do, and why do you do it?

ANSWER:_____

_____

_____

_____

_____

_____

2. You are ready for formation but your battle buddy is not. The Drill Sergeant promised he would make your lives a living hell if anyone is late for anything. You were told to be in formation, but you have also been taught to stick by your battle buddy. What do you do: help your battle buddy and take your chances on being late, or go to formation without him/her?

ANSWER:_____

_____

_____

_____

_____

_____

3. Your Drill Sergeant hits you. What do you do?

ANSWER:_____

_____

_____

_____

_____

_____

4. You are on a long run with your fellow recruits and you are trailing behind the rest of the pack. You know that if you slow down and walk for just a minute the rest of the run will be easier. The Drill Sergeants are all ahead of you, so the chances of them seeing you are very slim. What do you do?

ANSWER:_____

_____

_____

_____

_____

_____

5. Your Drill Sergeant asks you why you joined the military. How are you going to answer that question?

ANSWER:_____

_____

_____

_____

_____

_____

6. You notice that a fellow recruit leaves his wall locker unlocked and walks off to take a shower. What do you do?

ANSWER:_____

_____

_____

_____

_____

_____

7. It's Week 3 and your battle buddy hates basic training. He tells you he might injure himself or commit suicide to get out of his situation. What do you do?

ANSWER:_____

_____

_____

_____

_____

_____

8. You made a bad first impression in front of a Drill Sergeant. Every time he sees you he ridicules you and makes you do push ups. How do you handle this?

ANSWER:_____

_____

_____

_____

_____

_____

9. You have just arrived at basic training and a recruit seems to know everything the Drill Sergeants expect from him. He explains he has a long family military history and knows exactly how to handle Drill Sergeants and other boot camp situations. He tells you and other recruits to follow his lead. What do you do?

ANSWER:_____

_____

_____

_____

_____

Chapter 4

Matching

Follow the instructions below for each question. In general, you will be asked to match something (a string of text, a word, etc.) with the proper answer.

1. Each branch of basic training has one culminating event—an event a recruit will not forget. Match the culminating event with the proper branch:

Army/National Guard	A. Battle Stations
Navy	B. Victory Forge
Marines	C. Warrior Week
Air Force	D. Crucible

2. Match the branch of service with the appropriate characteristic:

Army/National Guard	A. Considered a rifleman first
Navy	B. Deep rooted with traditions and customs
Marines	C. Has 25 enlisted jobs to choose from
Coast Guard	D. Has hundreds of MOSs
Air Force	E. The most impressive technology / machinery

3. Match the branch of service with the appropriate award you receive when you graduate basic training or Advanced Individual Training (AIT):

Army/National Guard   A. ball cap
Navy   B. Eagle, Globe, and Anchor
Marines   C. service ribbon
Air Force   D. training ribbon

4. Match the letter answer below with the correct question:

— The number of smoke breaks you get per day at basic training.

— The number of suitcases you should pack for basic training.

— The percentage of women in the military.

— The number of degrees your feet should be apart at the position of attention.

— The percentage of all jobs in the military that are non-combat occupation.

   A. 45
   B. 80
   C. 20
   D. 0
   E. 1

5. Match the appropriate term with the appropriate branch of service:

Army/National Guard   A. Airman
Navy   B. Seaman
Marines   C. OohRah
Air Force   D. HUA

6. Match the appropriate time with the appropriate saying:

0001	A. Eleven hundred hours
0100	B. Ten hundred hours
1000	C. Zero one hundred hours
1100	D. Zero zero zero one

7. Match the appropriate military time with the corresponding civilian time:

0001	A. 10:00 a.m.
0100	B. 1:00 a.m.
1000	C. 12:01 a.m.
1100	D. 11:00 a.m.

8. Match the appropriate item of clothing with the order in which you would put the clothing on:

Put this item on first:	A. Pants
Put this item on second:	B. Boots
Put this item on third:	C. Socks
Put this item on last:	D. Brown t-shirt

9. Match the appropriate eating technique with the appropriate frequency you should perform the technique:

Always do this:	A. Choose brown rice
If given the option, always do this:	B. Drink plenty of water
Never do this:	C. Eat dessert
Do this as often as possible:	D. Make a sandwich out of your meals

10. Match the appropriate exercise with the appropriate nicknames you might hear a Drill Sergeant call them:

Deep knee bends	A. Ski jumpers
Running in place, hands on the ground	B. Donkey kicks
Hopping from side to side	C. Dusting your boots
Jumping, touch heels to buttocks	D. Mountain climbers

Chapter 5

Word Games: The Phonetic Alphabet

This chapter will teach you how to memorize the phonetic alphabet. Memorize the phonetic alphabet listed below, and then follow the instructions on the exercises in this chapter. After performing the exercises in this chapter, you will have every letter of the phonetic alphabet memorized.

The exercises in this chapter have been broken down and set up as flash cards. Using scissors, carefully cut the individual "cards" out of this book. Use them just as you would any flash cards. Have someone hold up one of the cards, and see how fast you can come up with the answer.

Do this over and over, keeping track of your time so you can determine whether you are improving, and how quickly.

Once you believe you mastered these words, wait a few days and then return and go through the exercise again, comparing your score to your previous best time. Did your time stay about the same, or did it worsen considerably? If the latter, you do not know the words as well as you believed.

Mastery of this phonetic alphabet will help you significantly during basic training.

Grab a pair of scissors and get moving!

Instructions

On the cards that follow, you will find the following information:

Letter	Phonetic Equivalent
A	Alpha
B	Bravo
C	Charlie
D	Delta
E	Echo
F	Foxtrot
G	Golf
H	Hotel
I	India
J	Juliet
K	Kilo
L	Lima
M	Mike
N	November
O	Oscar
P	Papa
Q	Quebec
R	Romeo
S	Sierra
T	Tango
U	Uniform
V	Victor
W	Whiskey
X	X-ray
Y	Yankee
Z	Zulu

Your job is to test yourself against yourself. If a card has the letter "O" on it, how quickly will it take you to say the name it stands for: "Oscar." That is your task. Good luck.

A	B
C	D
E	F
G	H

ALPHA	BRAVO
CHARLIE	DELTA
ECHO	FOXTROT
GOLF	HOTEL

I	J
K	L
M	N
O	P

INDIO	JULIET
KILO	LIMA
MIKE	NOVEMBER
OSCAR	PAPA

Q	R
S	T
U	V
W	X

QUEBEC	ROMEO
SIERRA	TANGO
UNIFORM	VICTOR
WHISKEY	X-RAY

Y	Z

YANKEE	ZULU

Here is another word exercise for you to try as you master the phonetic alphabet. Spell out the following words using the phonetic alphabet. For example:

Word: Pear (P-E-A-R)

Your Answer: Papa, Echo, Alpha, Romeo

Try not to look back at the list you just memorized. Go through the list at your own pace a few times, and then time yourself. Can you answer them all in five minutes? Four minutes? Two minutes? Sixty seconds? See how fast and accurately you can say the list, and keep trying to beat your previous time.

1. Button
*Answer:*_____

2. Flower
*Answer:*_____

3. Push
*Answer:*_____

4. City
*Answer:*_____

5. Zest
*Answer:*_____

6. Able
*Answer:*_____

7. Java

*Answer:*_____

8. Girl

*Answer:*_____

9. Quail

*Answer:*_____

10. Kind

*Answer:*_____

11. Deaf

*Answer:*_____

12. Mars

*Answer:*_____

13. Xerox®

*Answer:*_____

14. Happy

*Answer:*_____

15. Simple

*Answer:*_____

16. Extrude

*Answer:*_____

17. Fortify

*Answer:*_____

18. Army

*Answer:*_____

19. Navy

*Answer:*_____

20. Air Force

*Answer:*_____

21. Marines

*Answer:*_____

22. Coast Guard

*Answer:*_____

23. Chemical

*Answer:*_____

24. Ostrich

*Answer:*_____

25. Hydrogen

*Answer:*_____

Chapter 6

The Refrigerator Game

The following pages are intended to enhance and expand on your ability to memorize the phonetic alphabet with a memory-word association project. It will help you immensely if you memorize the phonetic alphabet <u>before</u> leaving for boot camp. By following this chapter <u>exactly</u>, step by step, you will enhance significantly your memorization of this alphabet.

Below you will find cut-out cards you can use to tape to certain items found in your home (the list matched to a letter provides a few examples of these items). Cut out the letter blocks that follow and tape them to items that begin with that letter of the alphabet. For example, tape the letter block A to an alarm clock, the letter B to a book, and so forth.

Keep these blocks taped to the items until you are confident that you have memorized that particular letter and word that goes along with it. Also, keep safety in mind: if you're looking for something for the letter I, try to avoid a hot iron!

A   Alarm clock, air freshener, aspirin
B   Books, bed
C   Couch, clock, coffee table, computer, chair
D   Door, dryer, drawer, DVD player, desk
E   Electronic device
F   Fan

G   Golf club, glass, garage door

H   Hair dryer

I   Iron

J   Jacket

K   Kitchen table

L   Light switch, lamp

M   Mirror, microwave

N   Nightstand

O   Oven door

P   Plant

Q

R   Refrigerator

S   Shower, stove

T   Television, toy, toaster

U   Umbrella

V   VCR, vitamin bottle

W   wall, washing machine, window

X

Y   Yardstick, yarn

Z   Zipper

A **ALPHA**	**B** **BRAVO**
C **CHARLIE**	**D** **DELTA**
E **ECHO**	**F** **FOXTROT**
G **GOLF**	**H** **HOTEL**

I **INDIA**	**J** **JULIET**
K **KILO**	**L** **LIMA**
M **MIKE**	**N** **NOVEMBER**
O **OSCAR**	**P** **PAPA**

Q **QUEBEC**	**R** **ROMEO**
S **SIERRA**	**T** **TANGO**
U **UNIFORM**	**V** **VICTOR**
W **WHISKEY**	**X** **X-RAY**

Y	Z
YANKEE	**ZULU**

Chapter 7

Ranks and Insignia

While all the chapters in this workbook are important and contribute positively to the experience you will have during basic training, pay special attention to this chapter on ranks and insignia.

This section displays the rank for each specific branch of the military. It will help you immensely if you *memorize* the ranks in the service you are entering *before* you leave for basic training. Study the charts, study the illustrations, and learn the ranks, in order.

If you can master this chapter—or even be a bit more than passingly familiar with it—you will be one <u>giant</u> leap ahead of the other recruits.

* * *

Army/National Guard Rank Structure

Army/National Guard Enlisted Rank			
Rank Insignia	Grade	Rank	Acronym
No rank insignia	E-1	Private	PV1
	E-2	Private	PV2
	E-3	Private First Class	PV3
	E-4	Corporal and Specialist	CPL, SPC
	E-5	Sergeant	SGT
	E-6	Staff Sergeant	SSG
	E-7	Sergeant First Class	SFC
	E-8	Master Sergeant and First Sergeant	MSG

Army/National Guard Warrant Officer Rank			
Rank Insignia	Grade	Rank	Acronym
	WO-1	Warrant Officer 1	WO-1
	CWO-2	Chief Warrant Officer 2	CW-2
	CWO-3	Chief Warrant Officer 3	CW-3
	CWO-4	Chief Warrant Officer 4	CW-4
	CWO-5	Chief Warrant Officer 5	CW-5
Army/National Guard Officer Rank			
(gold)	O-1	Second Lieutenant	2LT
(silver)	O-2	First Lieutenant	1LT

Army/National Guard Officer Rank (continued)			
Rank Insignia	Grade	Rank	Acronym
(two bars)	O-3	Captain	CPT
(gold)	O-4	Major	MAJ
(silver)	O-5	Lieutenant Colonel	LTC
(eagle)	O-6	Colonel	COL
(one star)	O-7	Brigadier General	BG
(two stars)	O-8	Major General	MG
(three stars)	O-9	Lieutenant General	LTG
(four stars)	O-10	General	GEN
(five stars)	O-11	General of the Army	GOA

Navy Rank Structure

Navy Enlisted Rank				
Pay Grade	Rank	Abbrev.	Upper Sleeve	Collar and Cap
E-1	Seaman Recruit	SR	None	None
E-2	Seaman Apprentice	SA		None
E-3	Seaman	SN		None
E-4	Petty Officer Third Class	PO3		
E-5	Petty Officer Second Class	PO2		
E-6	Petty Officer First Class	PO1		
E-7	Chief Petty Officer	CPO		
E-8	Senior Chief Petty Officer	SCPO		
E-9	Master Chief Petty Officer	MCPO		
E-10	Chief Petty Officer of the Navy	MCPON		

Navy Warrant Officer Rank

Pay Grade	Rank	Abbrev.	Collar	Shoulder	Sleeve
W-1	Chief Warrant Officer	CWO1			
W-2	Chief Warrant Officer	CWO2			
W-3	Chief Warrant Officer	CWO3			
W-4	Chief Warrant Officer	CWO4			

Navy Officer Rank

Pay Grade	Rank	Abbrev.	Collar	Shoulder	Sleeve
O-1	Ensign	ENS			
O-2	Lieutenant Junior Grade	LTJG			
O-3	Lieutenant	LT			
O-4	Lieutenant Commander	LCDR			

Navy Officer Rank (continued)					
Pay Grade	Rank	Abbrev.	Collar	Shoulder	Sleeve
O-5	Commander	CDR			
O-6	Captain	CAPT			
O-7	Rear Admiral	RDML			
O-8	Rear Admiral	RADM			
O-9	Vice Admiral	VADM			
O-10	Admiral	ADM			
O-11	Fleet Admiral	FADM			

Marine Rank Structure

Marine Enlisted Rank			
Rank Insignia	Grade	Rank	Acronym
No Rank Insignia	E-1	Private	PVT
	E-2	Private First Class	PFC
	E-3	Lance Corporal	LCpl
	E-4	Corporal	Cpl
	E-5	Sergeant	Sgt
	E-6	Staff Sergeant	SSgt
	E-7	Gunnery Sergeant	GySgt
	E-8	Master Sergeant	1stSgt
	E-8	First Sergeant	1stSgt

Marine Enlisted Rank (continued)			
Rank Insignia	Grade	Rank	Acronym
	E-9	Master Gunnery Sergeant	MGySgt
	E-9	Sergeant Major	SgtMaj
	E-9	Sergeant Major of the Marine Corps	SgtMaj

Marine Warrant Officer Rank			
Rank Insignia	Grade	Rank	Acronym
	WO-1	Warrant Officer 1	WO
	CWO-2	Chief Warrant Officer 2	CWO2
	CWO-3	Chief Warrant Officer 3	CWO3
	CWO-4	Chief Warrant Officer 4	CWO4
	CWO-5	Chief Warrant Officer 5	CWO5

Marine Officer Rank			
Rank Insignia	Grade	Rank	Acronym
(Gold)	O-1	Second Lieutenant	2LT
(Silver)	O-2	First Lieutenant	1LT
	O-3	Captain	CAPT
(gold)	O-4	Major	MAJ
(silver)	O-5	Lieutenant Colonel	LT COL
	O-6	Colonel	COL
	O-7	Brigadier General	BRIG GEN
	O-8	Major General	MAJ GEN
	O-9	Lieutenant General	LT GEN
	O-10	General	GEN

Air Force Rank Structure

Air Force Enlisted Rank			
Rank Insignia	Grade	Rank	Acronym
No Rank Insignia	E-1	Airman Basic	AB
	E-2	Airman	AMN
	E-3	Airman First Class	A1C
	E-4	Senior Airman	SrA
	E-5	Staff Sergeant	SSgt
	E-6	Technical Sergeant	TSgt
	E-7	Master Sergeant	MSgt
	E-8	Senior Master Sergeant	SMSgt
	E-9	Chief Master Sergeant	CMSgt
	E-9	Chief Master Sergeant of the Air Force	CMSAF

	Air Force Officer Rank		
Rank Insignia	Grade	Rank	Acronym
(gold)	O-1	Second Lieutenant	2 LT
(silver)	O-2	First Lieutenant	1 LT
	O-3	Captain	CAPT
(gold)	O-4	Major	MAJ
(silver)	O-5	Lieutenant Colonel	LT COL
	O-6	Colonel	COL
	O-7	Brigadier General	BRIG GEN
	O-8	Major General	MAJ GEN
	O-9	Lieutenant General	LT GEN
	O-10	General	GEN
	O-11	General of the Air Force	GEN

Coast Guard Rank Structure

Coast Guard Enlisted Rank			
Pay Grade	Rank	Abbreviation	Upper Sleeve
E-1	Seaman Recruit	SR	None
E-2	Seaman Apprentice	SA	
E-3	Seaman	SN	
E-4	Petty Officer Third Class	PO3	
E-5	Petty Officer Second Class	PO2	
E-6	Petty Officer First Class	PO1	
E-7	Chief Petty Officer	CPO	
E-8	Senior Chief Petty Officer	SCPO	
E-9	Master Chief Petty Officer	MCPO	
E-9	Master Chief Petty Officer of the Navy	MCPON	

Coast Guard Warrant Officer Rank			
Pay Grade	Rank	Abbreviation	Collar/Sleeve
W-2	Chief Warrant Officer	CWO2	
W-3	Chief Warrant Officer	CWO3	
W-4	Chief Warrant Officer	CWO4	

Coast Guard Officer Rank			
Pay Grade	Rank	Abbreviation	Collar/Sleeve
O-1	Ensign	ENS	(gold)
O-2	Lieutenant Junior Grade	LTJG	(silver)
O-3	Lieutenant	LT	
O-4	Lieutenant Commander	LCDR	(gold)
O-5	Commander	CDR	(silver)
O-6	Captain	CAPT	
O-7	Rear Admiral	RDML	

Coast Guard Officer Rank (continued)			
Pay Grade	Rank	Abbreviation	Collar/Sleeve
O-8	Rear Admiral	RADM	
O-9	Vice Admiral	VADM	
O-10	Admiral	ADM	
O-11	Fleet Admiral	FADM	

PART II

From Civilian to Military Fit: The Exercise Program
You Need to Succeed in Basic Training.

Chapter 8

"I learned that good judgment comes from experience and that experience grows out of mistakes." — General Omar N. Bradley

The Ultimate Basic Training Fitness Routine

The following workout routine (with some minor variations) can be found in *The Ultimate Basic Training Guidebook: Tips, Tricks and Tactics for Surviving Boot Camp* (Savas Beatie 2005). In this workbook you now hold in your hands, however, the workout logs have been reprinted to full size for your convenience and ease of use.

Please Note:

The fitness program presented in this book was not designed by a licensed physician. You should consult with a physician before beginning any fitness program or exercises discussed in this book. <u>All forms of exercise pose some inherent risk, even for people in top physical condition</u>. The author, and everyone who contributed to this book, advise readers to take full responsibility for their safety and know their limits and limitations. The statements (and illustrations) in this book are the opinion of the author.

A major portion of basic training focuses on building physical fitness and endurance. During basic training, your company will conduct an organized physical training session every morning, except Sundays. Each physical training session is comprised of three components:

- Warm-up;
- Conditioning;
- Cool-down.

Generally speaking, you will alternate between running days and push-up / sit-up days. You will find this effective in building your strength and stamina.

The Army measures your physical fitness and endurance by giving you multiple Army Physical Fitness Tests (APFT) throughout the nine-week basic training cycle. If you do not pass these tests, your Drill Sergeants will restart (recycle) you and you will be required to start basic training all over again.

The APFT has three components:

- Two-minute timed push-ups
- Two-minute timed sit-ups
- Two-mile timed run

You must score a minimum of 50 points in each category to pass an APFT. (Refer to the APFT charts in Appendix A. However, be aware that every so often the standards change.)

In Advanced Individual Training (AIT), which follows basic training, you must score a minimum of 60 points in each category to pass. It does not matter if you're an excellent runner and horrible at push-ups (or vice-versa). A maximum score in one category of an APFT (i.e., push-ups) does not affect the score of a different category (i.e., sit-ups). You must meet the minimum standards in each category. Even if you meet the minimum standards, your Drill Sergeants will not be pleased. You must surpass the minimum standards.

You should have no problem meeting the fitness standards by following the exercise program in this chapter for at least eight weeks prior to basic training. Again, Appendix A lists the APFT standards. The tables mentioned in this chapter are located in Appendix B.

Running Improvement

Running is the only fitness category in the APFT that tests your cardiovascular fitness. Most people have never learned to run properly. However, by learning and applying a few simple techniques, the efficiency of your body movements can increase dramatically. Always try to run with a partner; it is motivating and easier to keep pace with someone running next to you. Just make sure your partner doesn't slow you down. During the APFT, you may choose to run with a partner or alone.

The running program in this chapter is to be performed every other day. You will alternate between sprint days and long-run days. By following this program at least eight weeks prior to basic training, you should have no problems passing (or even maxing) the running portion of the APFT.

Selecting the Proper Running Shoe

The first step in finding the proper running shoe is to determine your foot type. There are three main types of feet: high arch, normal arch, and low arch. To determine which type you are, wet your feet thoroughly and shake off the excess water. Next, step on a dark and dry surface. I recommend a brown paper bag or a piece of smooth wood. The imprint produced will form a shape similar to one of the three shown below in Figure 1:

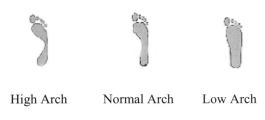

High Arch   Normal Arch   Low Arch

Figure 1: Foot Shapes

Once you determine which foot type you are, you can shop for the proper running shoe. Don't shop for shoes in the morning; your feet swell slightly when you sleep, which could give you a false assumption of your actual foot size.

If you have a highly arched foot, you need a shoe with extra cushioning in the middle area of the shoe (Army and Air Force Exchange Service [AAFES] tag "C").

If you have a normal foot type, your ankles pronate inward as you step. Therefore you will need a shoe with average cushioning (AAFES tag "S"). Do not buy a shoe with extra cushioning in one area or extra motion control features.

If you have a low arched foot, your ankles pronate inward, but more excessively than the normal foot type. Buy a straight or slightly curved shoe, such as a motion control shoe (AAFES tag "M"). AAFES tagged shoes can be found at Post Exchanges (PX).

Figure 2: Common mistake when stretching the quadriceps.

Stretching

Always stretch before you do any physical exercise. The following stretching techniques will help you properly prepare your body for running:

Quadriceps
(front top of the leg)

Balance yourself against a sturdy object or wall. Grasp your right ankle behind your back with your right hand. Gently pull up with your hand. Figure 2 (on the left) shows a common mistake many people make when trying to perform this stretch. Be sure to pull at the ankle and not pull at the toes. Doing this will reduce the chance of an injury. Keep your head up, stand erect, and do not bend over at the waist. Do not bounce. Hold this stretch for a minimum of thirty seconds for each leg.

Groin Stretch (inner legs)

With your buttocks on the floor place the bottom of your feet together in front of you (Figure 3, below). Slowly bring your feet as close to your body as possible. Gently grasp your feet and slowly push your knees toward the floor with your elbows. Hold this stretch for a minimum of 30 seconds.

Figure 3: Proper technique for stretching the groin.

Hamstrings (back of legs)

With your buttocks on the floor, straighten your legs in front of you about 18" apart (Figure 4, next page).

Figure 4: Proper technique for stretching the hamstrings.

Gently reach for the toe on your right leg with your right arm, and hold this for about thirty seconds. When you are finished, repeat this with the left leg, and hold again for about thirty seconds. This simple exercise will stretch the hamstrings, <u>but do it gently</u> <u>and slowly, so you do not risk injuring your lower back or pulling a different set of muscles</u>.

Calves
(back and bottom of legs)

Lean against a wall with the left leg behind you as shown in Figure 5 (left). The right leg should be in front of you bearing most of your weight. Keep the heel of the left foot on the floor with the toe pointed forward. Gently move your hips forward toward the wall. The farther forward your hips move, the greater the stretch. Hold for 30 seconds and repeat with the other leg.

Figure 5: Proper technique for stretching the calves.

Running Technique

Before you begin any running program, you must learn how to run properly. By practicing the various running techniques outlined here, you will greatly improve your efficiency and reduce the risk of injury.

Below is a list of quick fix running tips you can implement immediately into your running program. If you find that these techniques change your stride significantly, then make

> **Did you Know?**
>
> A stride is calculated by measuring the distance of ten normal sized steps, and dividing the distance you walked by 10.

your changes gradually. These new techniques could put stress on different muscle groups, which could result in injury until your body adapts to the new running style.

Quick Fix #1

Run straight in a vertical alignment. Your body should be angled forward to the point where you will almost feel like falling over. Be careful not to stick your buttocks out; doing so will create improper balance.

Quick Fix #2

Keep your feet on the ground as little as possible. It is common for people to run heel to toe as their foot strikes the ground. Land on the mid-foot, or forefoot if possible. When you land on your heels, you are placing your body's center of gravity behind you. This forces your body to push harder with every step and wastes energy.

Quick Fix #3

Do not bounce when you run. Use your energy to create horizontal and not vertical movement. The less vertical movement you have when running, the more energy you can use to propel your body forward.

Quick Fix #4

Your foot should land under your body when it strikes the ground, not in front of you. By doing this, you will ensure better leverage and balance.

Quick Fix #5

Don't swing your legs back and forth. Instead, when your foot strikes the ground, pull your heel toward your butt by contracting the hamstring. This technique creates a shorter leg arch so your legs get in position faster for the next step without any wasted energy.

Quick Fix #6

Resist the temptation to push off with your toes. By contracting your hamstring muscles (as described in quick fix #5) you will save energy for those long runs.

Summary

Quick Fix #1: Run straight in a
vertical alignment.

Quick Fix #2: Keep your feet on the
ground as little as possible.

Quick Fix #3: Don't bounce when you run.

Quick Fix #4: Your foot should land under
your body when it strikes the ground.

Quick Fix #5: Pull your heel toward your
buttocks by contracting the hamstring.

Quick Fix #6: Resist the temptation
to push off with your toes.

8-Week Running Program

Running should be done every other day. Getting sufficient rest is just as important as exercising. Resting allows your body to recuperate and allows your muscles to get stronger after a workout.

This running program can be accomplished regardless of your current fitness level. If you find this program too easy, then add some distance and/or speed to the run. Just make sure that you follow the minimum requirements.

This program gives you eight weeks to get in shape for basic training. If you have more time than eight weeks, then take advantage and begin early. If you don't have eight weeks to complete this program, start from the beginning and do what you can.

Every little bit helps before you start basic training.

Warm-Up With a Jump Rope

Jumping rope is a great warm-up exercise. It gets your blood flowing, your heart rate up, and your muscles ready for the run. Jumping rope also builds the lower leg muscles that are essential for running. A proper warm-up is outlined in Table 1 and should be followed before every run. If the jump rope gets tangled and you are forced to restart your movement, add the time you stopped jumping to the time limit you are trying to accomplish.

Initial Assessment

This running program will increase your running distance and improve your running speed. Don't ever fall behind in a run in basic training. If you do, your Drill Sergeant will believe you are unmotivated, and you could lose privileges (such as passes). Before you begin this running program, you need to evaluate your level of fitness. You will need a stopwatch and a pedometer to do so.

A pedometer is a device that attaches to your hip and calculates how far you have run. A pedometer can be purchased at just about any sports store for a few dollars. If you are running on a

Equipment Needed:

- Stop Watch

- Pedometer

You can either push yourself hard on your own terms . . .

standard track, a pedometer is not needed. One complete circle around a standard track is one-quarter (¼) mile, or 440 yards.

After you have stretched and elevated your heart rate with jump rope exercises, you can begin your assessment. Use your stopwatch and determine how long it took you to run one mile. One mile equals four laps around a standard track. Look in Appendice 1 and determine the minimum time you will need on the APFT (use the 50-point mark). Insert that time in Table 2.

Complete the one-mile run as fast as possible. Log this one-mile run on all three dotted lines in Table 2. Be sure to log your time in seconds. For example, an 8:36 minute one-mile run equals 516 seconds. Next, fill in the blanks to determine your "sprint time goal." The .80 will increase your one-mile jog time by 20 percent.

Since this might be your first time running in a while, do whatever it takes to keep running. Absolutely resist the urge to walk. When you alternate running and walking, your body (and your heart) will not be able to maintain a consistent rate. If you absolutely must stop running, then walk briskly. You need to keep your heart rate up to increase your fitness level. Stop if you feel pain.

. . . or be forced to push yourself on your Drill Sergeant's terms.

Just remember: push yourself hard on your own terms, or be forced to push yourself on your Drill Sergeant's terms. Take a one-day rest after the one-mile assessment.

Sprint Day

Initially, run ¼-mile. Be sure to beat the sprint time goal (from Table 2). If you run ¼-mile and do not beat the goal, then re-run the ¼-mile. It might sound tough, but again, better to be disciplined on your own terms than on your Drill Sergeant's terms. Once you complete a ¼-mile run, then walk briskly for ¼-mile. You want to keep your heart rate up to increase your stamina. Log your time in Set 1 on Table 3.

After the ¼-mile brisk walk, complete a second ¼-mile sprint, log this time under Set 2. Again, walk briskly for ¼-mile. Repeat three more times until you have completed all five sets. After completion, be sure to stretch and drink water. After two weeks, fill in the evaluation chart (Table 4). Only use the run times in which you surpassed your sprint time goal. If you did not surpass your goal, use the "re-done laps" time instead. Remember, the "re-done laps" are those ¼-mile laps you had to redo because you failed to surpass your sprint time goal.

Once you complete Tables 3 and 4, continue your running program by completing Tables 5 and 6, Tables 7 and 8, and Tables 9 and 10. With each set of tables completed, your sprint goal is calculated (by filling in the evaluation chart) to be 10 percent faster than the previous two weeks. Once the tables are completed, run two miles to the best of your ability. Refer back to Table 2 and compare your new two-mile score with the APFT standard. You will be amazed at the improvement. Be sure to keep an accurate log with the tables. Charting your progress is important and motivational.

Long-Run Day

On long-run days, your goal is to keep your heart rate up for a measured period of time. If your legs are sore, don't run. Replace running with stretching your legs. Be sure to focus on the running techniques outlined in the beginning of this chapter. Follow Table 11 during long-run days. You are running for a length of time during this session and not necessarily for speed, as you do during sprint days. If you cannot continue running, stop the stopwatch and walk briskly. Continue the stopwatch once you begin running again. Since you are performing the running program every other day, you should alternate between sprint days and long run days.

Did You Know?

The one-quarter billion skeletal muscle fibers in your body can be categorized as two main types?

Type 1 fibers are used for endurance activities.

Type 2 fibers are used when a task utilizes more than 25% of your maximum strength.

The human body is truly an amazing creation!

Push-Up Improvement

The push-up is used by the Army to test your upper body strength. There are literally hundreds of exercises you can do to build upper body strength. However,

Figure 6: Proper push-up form—starting position.

the best way to increase the number of push-ups you can do in two minutes is to actually DO the push-ups.

The push-up program I have set forth below should be performed every other day, along with the sit-up program. Note, however, that practicing both push-ups and sit-ups too often does not allow for muscle recuperation.

Figure 6 (above) shows the proper starting position for a push-up. Notice the back and legs are straight, the head is up and the arms are at shoulder level. Your body should be lowered to the position as shown in Figure7 (below). The upper arms are parallel to the floor and the back and legs remain straight.

Figure 7: Proper Push-up form—lowered position.

Stretching for Push-Ups

The push-up involves numerous upper body muscles, primarily the triceps, chest, and the shoulders. By stretching these muscles before each workout, you will reduce your muscle soreness and your chance of injury.

Triceps (back of arm)

Lift your right arm up over your head with your left hand pushing back on the right triceps just above your right elbow (Figure 8, to the right). Hold for thirty seconds and repeat with the left arm. This also stretches the shoulders.

Chest

Position your forearm on the edge of a wall or other stationary object (Figure 9, next page). Place your feet in line with the wall's edge. Lean out and away from the wall's edge. Hold for a minimum of thirty seconds then repeat with the other arm.

Figure 8: Proper technique for stretching the triceps.

Shoulders

Place your right arm behind your back with your right hand reaching toward your left shoulder, as shown in Figure 10 (next page). Grab your right wrist with your left hand and pull it gently higher. Hold for thirty seconds, then repeat with left arm.

Figure 9: Proper technique for stretching the chest.

Figure 10: Proper technique for stretching the shoulders.

Improving Push-Up Performance

This push-up program is designed to be rigorous, regardless of your current fitness level. The more you put into this program, the more you will get out of it. You will be doing both fast and slow push-ups.

Refer to Appendix 1 to determine the number of push-ups you must complete to pass the APFT (use the 50-point mark). Enter that number at the top of Table 12. After proper stretching, see how many push-ups you can do in one minute. Do these push-ups as quickly as possible, but in a controlled manner. Only those push-ups with correct form should be counted. Remember the number of push-ups you just performed. Drop immediately to your knees and continue doing push-ups, but this time put your hands close together (as shown in Figure 11 below). This type of push-up is called a kneeling diamond push-up because your forefinger and thumbs form a diamond shape. These push-ups should be done very slowly—three seconds for the downward movement, and three seconds for the upward movement.

Keep doing push-ups until you can't continue. When you are done, enter your numbers in line A and B in Set 1 of Table 12 (enter A for regular push-ups and B for kneeling diamond push-ups). Rest two full minutes and complete another set.

Figure 11: Proper technique for kneeling diamond push-up.

Enter those numbers in Table 12, Set 2, lines A and B. Complete a third set and stretch afterward. After three weeks of performing three sets of one-minute timed push-ups, complete three weeks of 1:30 minute timed push-ups. For weeks Seven and Eight, do three sets of two-minute timed push-ups. Perform this workout every other day along with the sit-up program.

<u>Do not be discouraged if by the second or third set your number does not meet the minimum APFT standards.</u> Your muscles will be tired before the sets even start, unlike when you take an APFT test when your muscles are fresh. By the time basic training starts, you will be prepared to meet and exceed the push-up standard.

Sit-Up Improvement

Figure 12 (below) shows the proper starting position for a sit-up. Notice the legs are bent at a 90-degree angle, the heel is in contact with the floor, and the fingers are interlocked behind the head. During an APFT, a partner will be holding your ankles with his hands. Your body should be raised to the position as shown in Figure 13 (next page). In the vertical position, the base of the neck is above the base of the spine.

Figure 12: Proper sit-up form (starting position).

During an APFT, raising your body to the vertical position and returning it to the lowered position is considered one full repetition. Similar to the push-up, you can save considerable energy during a fitness test by using gravity to let your body return to the lowered position. However, during practice you can build muscular endurance by lowering yourself slowly to the starting position.

Figure 13: Proper sit-up form (vertical position).

This sit-up program is intense, so <u>stop immediately</u> if you feel any abnormal discomfort, and rest and reduce the intensity.

Stretching for Sit-Ups

The sit-up involves the torso and abdominal muscles. Soldiers often injure their upper quadriceps (leg muscles) by using the wrong muscles to raise them to a vertical position. To thoroughly stretch before a sit-up, perform the stretch described for quadriceps in the running section. Note: sit-ups done improperly can be harmful to the back. The torso extension stretch as shown in Figure 14 (next page, top image) will stretch your abdominal muscles and the spine.

To properly perform the torso extension stretch, lie on your stomach and use your forearms to hold your body weight. Relax and slowly raise your upper body, keeping your waist on the floor. Hold for a minimum of thirty seconds. To increase the intensity of the stretch, place the palms of your hands on the floor, instead of your forearms.

Figure 14: Torso extension stretch.

Improving Sit-Up Performance

This eight-week sit-up program is designed to significantly increase the amount of sit-ups you can do in two minutes. This program is not designed to give you a flat six-pack stomach or melt inches off your waist.

Perform this program on the same day as the push-up program. Before starting, get comfortable by placing a towel under your tail bone or use a soft surface, such as a mat, to lie on. Do not use a bulky surface such as a couch or mattress.

Refer to Appendix 1 to determine the amount of sit-ups you will need to do to pass your fitness test (use the 50-point mark). Enter that number at the top of Table 13. After proper stretching, see how many sit-ups you can perform in one minute. Do these sit-ups as quickly as possible and with correct form. Breathe out on the

Figure 15: Proper technique for abdominal crunches.

Figure 16: Proper technique for upper half crunches.

way up. Remember the number of sit-ups you just performed. Immediately begin abdominal crunches (as shown in Figure 15, previous page). Place your hands behind your head or across your chest. Once your shoulder blades are off the ground, return to the starting position. Perform abdominal crunches until you cannot continue. When you are done, enter your numbers in line A and B in Set 1 of Table 13 (A for regular sit-ups and B for abdominal crunches). Rest two full minutes and complete another set.

This time, instead of performing abdominal crunches, perform upper-half crunches. The mid-point of the sit-up is the starting position for this exercise (Figure 16, above). Enter those numbers in Table 13, Set 2, lines A and C. After three weeks of performing two sets of one-minute timed sit-ups, complete three weeks of 1:30 minute timed sit-ups. For the seventh and eighth weeks, do two sets of two-minute timed sit-ups. Once this eight-week sit-up improvement program is complete, APFT standards will be easily accomplished.

Table 14 outlines exactly what you need to accomplish, day-by-day, for eight weeks. Use Table 14 as a checklist. If you are unable to workout for a day, <u>do not skip the workout</u>! Instead, use it as a day of rest, and pick up the exercise program the next day where you left off.

Tips for Maximizing Your APFT Score

- During an APFT, lowering your body and raising it to the starting position is considered one full repetition. Save energy during a fitness test by using gravity to let your body fall. However, during practice you will want to lower your body in a controlled manner to build muscle.

- When taking an APFT, you may have to wait in a long line before it is time to perform your push-ups or sit-ups. About five minutes before it's your turn, perform just a few push-ups or sit-ups (depending on which portion of the test you're waiting to take). Doing this will increase your blood flow and prepare your muscles for the task at hand.

- Avoid muscle failure during an APFT when doing the push-ups and sit-ups. When your muscles approach failure, rest for a little while, and then start back up again. Be sure to rest in an authorized position, which will be explained to you before the APFT begins.

- Sometimes an APFT grader will not count a repetition for various reasons (i.e., didn't come up high enough on a sit-up, or down far enough on a push-up). When this happens, make a deliberate and obvious attempt to correct your form. Doing this will let the grader know that you heard his remark and the problem is being rectified. Always focus on form. Try not to waste energy on bad repetitions.

- Pace your breathing and speed on the running portion of the test. Many recruits get anxious during the run and take off running full speed (or nearly full speed) when the whistle blows. There are many reasons why you should avoid doing this. By starting slow on the run, you will be passing others one-half mile down the road, which is motivational.

Miscellaneous Exercises

Other than push-ups and sit-ups, there are several miscellaneous exercises you will need to know about before arriving at basic training. Some exercises you do in basic training are common knowledge, such as jumping jacks, military presses (using your eight-pound —16 rifle as a weight), and pull-ups. In basic training, you won't go to a gym and lift weights. Many exercises you do will use your body weight as resistance. This is a good reason to lose weight before basic training starts.

In basic training, you will become very familiar with the following exercises. Practice these exercises at home until you are familiar with the form.

Flutterkicks: Strengthens the Stomach

Lie on your back and place your hands under your buttocks. Raise your feet six inches above the ground with your legs very slightly bent and head off the ground as shown in Figure 17 (below). This is your starting position. To begin the movement, raise one of your legs about 12 to 16 inches. As that leg reaches the top, begin returning it to the starting position as you raise the other leg 12 to 16 inches. Repeat.

Figure 17: Starting position of a flutterkick.

Overhead Claps: Strengthens the Shoulders

Extend both your arms to the side of your body, about shoulder level with your palms facing up as shown in Figure 18 (next page). Your arms should be bent slightly. Raise your arms up and clap your hands above your head. Return them to the starting position and repeat.

Planks: Strengthens the Stomach

Assume the push-up position. Instead of resting on your hands, rest on your forearms (Figure 19, page 101). Your back should be straight. Hold this position

Figure 18: Starting position of overhead claps.

for one minute. After about twenty seconds you will feel your abdominal muscles getting tight. The further you bring your elbows past your head, the more difficult this exercise will become.

Leg Spreaders: Strengthens the Inner Thighs

Assume the flutterkick starting position. Keep your legs slightly bent to reduce back strain. Spread your legs approximately 18 to 30 inches apart. Return your legs to the starting position and repeat.

Figure 19: Starting position of a plank.

Ski Jumpers: Strengthens the Legs and Calves

Stand upright, place your hands on top of your head, and your feet together. Jump to the left about 18 inches. As soon as you touch the ground, jump to the right about 18 inches. Repeat. The faster you perform this exercise, the more challenging it will become.

Front-Back-Go: Strengthens the Cardiovascular System

You will need a partner for this exercise. When your partner yells "front," you will begin doing push-ups as fast as possible. After you do push-ups for a while, have your partner yell "back." On the command of "back" you will start doing sit-ups as fast as possible. After some time elapses, have your partner yell "go!" On the command "Go!" you will run in place with your arms extended in front of you. Your Drill Sergeant will certainly get you acquainted with this exercise.

Toe Touches: Strengthens the Legs

Stand upright with your feet shoulder width apart. Place your hands on your hips. This is the starting position. Begin by bending your legs and touching your ankles. Keep your back straight. Return to the starting position and repeat. Drill Sergeants often refer to this exercise as "dusting your boots."

Donkey Kicks: Strengthens the Legs and Cardiovascular System

Stand upright and interlock your fingers behind your head. This is your starting position. Jump and kick your heels to your buttocks. Repeat. This exercise, also called "mule kicks," is commonly done on gravel and sand to increase difficulty.

Figure 20: Starting position of mountain climbers.

Mountain Climbers: Strengthens the Legs and the Cardiovascular System

Place your hands on the ground approximately three or four feet in front of your feet. Your back should be naturally arched (Figure 20, above). This is the starting position.

Begin the exercise by running in place without moving your hands. Move your knees close to your chest.

Appendix 1

Workout Logs

Full size downloadable workout logs are also available online exclusively at www.ultimatebasictrainingguidebook.com. An explanation on how to use Tables 3-10 can be found in Chapter 8 under the Sprint Day subsection.

To properly follow Table 11, remember, you are running for a length of time not necessarily for speed.

An explanation on how to use Tables 12 and 13 can be found in Chapter 8 under the Improving Push-Up Performance and Improving Sit-Up Performance subsection, respectively.

Use Table 14 as a checklist. This table outlines exactly what you need to accomplish, day-by-day, for eight weeks. If you are unable to workout for a day, do not skip the workout, just use it as a day of rest and pick up where you left off the next day.

Table 1. Jump Rope Program			
Weeks 1 and 2		**Weeks 3 and 4**	
Time Limit	Style	Time Limit	Style
1 minute	feet together	2 minutes	feet together
rest 45 seconds		rest 45 seconds	
1 minute	feet together	2 minutes	alternating legs
rest 45 seconds		rest 45 seconds	
2 minutes	feet together	1 minute	left foot only
		rest 45 seconds	
		1 minute	right foot only
Weeks 5 and 6		**Weeks 7 and 8**	
Time Limit	Style	Time Limit	Style
2:30 minutes	feet together	3:00 minutes	feet together
rest 1 minute		rest 1 minute	
2:30 minutes	alternating legs	3:00 minutes	feet together
rest 1 minute		rest 1 minute	
1:30 minute	left foot only	2:00 minutes	feet together
rest 1 minute		rest 1 minute	
1:30 minute	right foot only	2:00 minutes	feet together

Table 2. Initial Running Assessment

Date: _____

Minimum APFT Score: _____
                                    Time (seconds)

1-mile assessment   = _ _ _ _ _

Estimated 2-mile assessment = _ _ _ _ _ x2=_____

1/4-mile sprint time goal   = _ _ _ _ _ /4=_____ x.80=_____

Table 3. Sprint Day Log (Weeks 1 and 2)

_____ Sprint Time Goal (carried over from Table 2)

Date	Sprint	Goal Beat?	Sprint	Goal Beat?	Sprint	Goal Beat?
Set 1						
Set 2						
Set 3						
Set 4						
Set 5						
re-done laps						
re-done laps						

Date	Sprint	Goal Beat?	Sprint	Goal Beat?	Sprint	Goal Beat?
Set 1						
Set 2						
Set 3						
Set 4						
Set 5						
re-done laps						
re-done laps						

Date	Sprint	Goal Beat?	Sprint	Goal Beat?	Sprint	Goal Beat?
Set 1						
Set 2						
Set 3						
Set 4						
Set 5						
re-done laps						
re-done laps						

Table 4. Evaluation Chart (Weeks 1 and 2)

_____ Sum of set 1 from Table 3 (in seconds)	divided by	_____ Number of times you completed set 1	X	0.9	___ A
_____ Sum of set 2 from Table 3 (in seconds)	divided by	_____ Number of times you completed set 2	X	0.9	___ B
_____ Sum of set 3 from Table 3 (in seconds)	divided by	_____ Number of times you completed set 3	X	0.9	___ C
_____ Sum of set 4 from Table 3 (in seconds)	divided by	_____ Number of times you completed set 4	X	0.9	___ D
_____ Sum of set 5 from Table 3 (in seconds)	divided by	_____ Number of times you completed set 5	X	0.9	___ E

$A + B + C + D + E / 5$ =   _____ New Sprint Time Goal

Table 5. Sprint Day Log (Weeks 3 and 4)

_____ Sprint Time Goal (carried over from Table 4)

Date	Sprint	Goal Beat?	Sprint	Goal Beat?	Sprint	Goal Beat?
Set 1						
Set 2						
Set 3						
Set 4						
Set 5						
Set 6						
re-done laps						
re-done laps						

Date	Sprint	Goal Beat?	Sprint	Goal Beat?	Sprint	Goal Beat?
Set 1						
Set 2						
Set 3						
Set 4						
Set 5						
Set 6						
re-done laps						
re-done laps						

Table 6. Evaluation Chart (Weeks 3 and 4)

_____	divided by	_____	X	0.9	___	A
Sum of set 1 from Table 5 (in seconds)		Number of times you completed set 1				
_____	divided by	_____	X	0.9	___	B
Sum of set 2 from Table 5 (in seconds)		Number of times you completed set 2				
_____	divided by	_____	X	0.9	___	C
Sum of set 3 from Table 5 (in seconds)		Number of times you completed set 3				
_____	divided by	_____	X	0.9	___	D
Sum of set 4 from Table 5 (in seconds)		Number of times you completed set 4				
_____	divided by	_____	X	0.9	___	E
Sum of set 5 from Table 5 (in seconds)		Number of times you completed set 5				
_____	divided by	_____	X	0.9	___	F
Sum of set 6 from Table 5 (in seconds)		Number of times you completed set 6				

A + B + C + D + E + F / 6   =   _____   New Sprint Time Goal

Table 7. Sprint Day Log (Weeks 5 and 6)

_____   Sprint Time Goal (carried over from Table 6)

Date	Sprint Goal Beat?		Sprint Goal Beat?		Sprint Goal Beat?	
Set 1						
Set 2						
Set 3						
Set 4						
Set 5						
Set 6						
Set 7						
re-done laps						
re-done laps						

Date	Sprint Goal Beat?		Sprint Goal Beat?		Sprint Goal Beat?	
Set 1						
Set 2						
Set 3						
Set 4						
Set 5						
Set 6						
Set 7						
re-done laps						
re-done laps						

Table 8. Evaluation Chart (Weeks 5 and 6)

_____ Sum of set 1 from Table 7 (in seconds)	divided by	_____ Number of times you completed set 1	X	0.9	_____	A
_____ Sum of set 2 from Table 7 (in seconds)	divided by	_____ Number of times you completed set 2	X	0.9	_____	B
_____ Sum of set 3 from Table 7 (in seconds)	divided by	_____ Number of times you completed set 3	X	0.9	_____	C
_____ Sum of set 4 from Table 7 (in seconds)	divided by	_____ Number of times you completed set 4	X	0.9	_____	D
_____ Sum of set 5 from Table 7 (in seconds)	divided by	_____ Number of times you completed set 5	X	0.9	_____	E
_____ Sum of set 6 from Table 7 (in seconds)	divided by	_____ Number of times you completed set 6	X	0.9	_____	F
_____ Sum of set 7 from Table 7 (in seconds)	divided by	_____ Number of times you completed set 7	X	0.9	_____	G

$A + B + C + D + E + F + G / 7$ =   _____   New Sprint Time Goal

Table 9. Sprint Day Log (Weeks 7 and 8)

_____ Sprint Time Goal (carried over from Table 8)

Date	Sprint	Goal Beat?	Sprint	Goal Beat?	Sprint	Goal Beat?
Set 1						
Set 2						
Set 3						
Set 4						
Set 5						
Set 6						
Set 7						
Set 8						
re-done laps						
re-done laps						

Date	Sprint	Goal Beat?	Sprint	Goal Beat?	Sprint	Goal Beat?
Set 1						
Set 2						
Set 3						
Set 4						
Set 5						
Set 6						
Set 7						
Set 8						
re-done laps						
re-done laps						

Table 10. Evaluation Chart (Weeks 7 and 8)

_____ divided by _____ X 0.9 ____ A
Sum of set 1 from / Number of times you completed set 1
Table 9 (in seconds)

_____ divided by _____ X 0.9 ____ B
Sum of set 2 from / Number of times you completed set 2
Table 9 (in seconds)

_____ divided by _____ X 0.9 ____ C
Sum of set 3 from / Number of times you completed set 3
Table 9 (in seconds)

_____ divided by _____ X 0.9 ____ D
Sum of set 4 from / Number of times you completed set 4
Table 9 (in seconds)

_____ divided by _____ X 0.9 ____ E
Sum of set 5 from / Number of times you completed set 5
Table 9 (in seconds)

_____ divided by _____ X 0.9 ____ F
Sum of set 6 from / Number of times you completed set 6
Table 9 (in seconds)

_____ divided by _____ X 0.9 ____ G
Sum of set 7 from / Number of times you completed set 7
Table 9 (in seconds)

_____ divided by _____ X 0.9 ____ H
Sum of set 8 from / Number of times you completed set 8
Table 9 (in seconds)

A + B + C + D + E + F + G + H / 8   = _____ New Sprint Time Goal

Table 11. Running Program for Long-Run Days

Run for a minimum of:

Week 1 20:00 minutes/day

Week 2 22:00 minutes/day

Week 3 24:00 minutes/day

Week 4 26:30 minutes/day

Week 5 28:30 minutes/day

Week 6 31:00 minutes/day

Week 7 33:30 minutes/day

Week 8 36:00 minutes/day

Table 12. Push-up Evaluation Chart

_____ Number of push-ups required to pass APFT

Rest	2 minutes between sets							
Wks 1-3	Duration	Day 1	Day 2	Day 3	Day 4	Day 5	Day 6	Day 7
Set 1	A* 1-minute	___	___	___	___	___	___	___
	B* failure	___	___	___	___	___	___	___
Set 2	A 1-minute	___	___	___	___	___	___	___
	B failure	___	___	___	___	___	___	___
Set 3	A 1-minute	___	___	___	___	___	___	___
	B failure	___	___	___	___	___	___	___
Rest	3 minutes between sets							
Wks 4-6	Duration	Day 1	Day 2	Day 3	Day 4	Day 5	Day 6	Day 7
Set 1	1:30							
	A minutes	___	___	___	___	___	___	___
	B failure	___	___	___	___	___	___	___
Set 2	1:30							
	A minutes	___	___	___	___	___	___	___
	B failure	___	___	___	___	___	___	___
Set 3	1:30							
	A minutes	___	___	___	___	___	___	___
	B failure	___	___	___	___	___	___	___
Rest	4 minutes between sets							
Wks 7-8	Duration	Day 1	Day 2	Day 3	Day 4	Day 5	Day 6	Day 7
Set 1	A 2-minutes	___	___	___	___	___	___	___
	B failure	___	___	___	___	___	___	___
Set 2	A 2-minutes	___	___	___	___	___	___	___
	B failure	___	___	___	___	___	___	___
Set 3	A 2-minutes	___	___	___	___	___	___	___
	B failure	___	___	___	___	___	___	___

A*regular push-ups
B*kneeling diamond push-ups

Table 13. Sit-up Evaluation Chart

_____ Number of sit-ups required to pass APFT

Rest	2 minutes between sets							
Weeks 1-3	Duration	Day 1	Day 2	Day 3	Day 4	Day 5	Day 6	Day 7
Set 1	A* 1-minute							
	B* failure							
Set 2	A 1-minute							
	C* failure							
Rest	3 minutes between sets							
Weeks 4-6	Duration	Day 1	Day 2	Day 3	Day 4	Day 5	Day 6	Day 7
Set 1	A 1:30 minutes							
	B failure							
Set 2	A 1:30 minutes							
	C failure							
Rest	4 minutes between sets							
Weeks 7-8	Duration	Day 1	Day 2	Day 3	Day 4	Day 5	Day 6	Day 7
Set 1	A 2-minutes							
	B failure							
Set 2	A 2-minutes							
	C failure							

A*regular sit-ups
B*abdominal crunches
C*upper-half crunches

Table 14. 8-Week Fitness Chart							
	Week 1	Week 2	Week 3	Week 4	Week 5	Week 6	Week 7	Week 8
Day 1	A	B	C (24 m)	B	D	B	C (33:30 m)	B
Day 2	B	D	B	C (26:30 m)	B	D	B	C (36 m)
Day 3	C (20 m)	B	D	B	C (28:30 m)	B	D	B
Day 4	B	C (22 m)	B	D	B	C (31 m)	B	D
Day 5	D	B	C (24 m)	B	D	B	C (33:30 m)	B
Day 6	B	D	B	C (26:30 m)	B	D	B	C (36 m)
Day 7	C (20 m)	B	D	B	C (28:30 m)	B (31 m)	D	B

A   1-mile assessment   m   minutes

B   push-ups and sit-ups

C   long run day

D   sprint day

Appendix 2

Army/National Guard Fitness Charts

How to Read the Army/National Guard Physical Fitness Charts

Find your age bracket in the top row of each table (Tables 15, 16, and 17), and then find the column for your gender under that age bracket. For example, if you are a 23-year-old male, you will find age category 22-26. In that column is the letter M (male) and the letter F (female). For this example we will reference the M column. As you can see in the push-up standard chart, the number 100 corresponds to the number 75 in the repetitions column to the left. This means, in order to score a perfect 100 on your push-up test, you will need to do 75 push-ups in a two-minute period. You will always get two minutes for both the push-up and sit-up fitness tests.

In the Army, if you fail any of the three fitness tests (push-ups, sit-ups, or the run) you fail the entire test. After you graduate basic training, you will be required to score at least a 60 in each category. You will want to score at least a 60 in each category. If you score a 100 on the sit-up test, that doesn't mean you can score less than a 60 on the push-up test. You must score at least a 60 in each category to pass the fitness test.

To reiterate: for a 23-year-old male, the following standards must be surpassed to pass a fitness test in basic training: 40 push-ups / 50 sit-ups / 16:36 two-mile timed run.

Table 15. Army Push-Up Standard*

Repetitions	17-21 M	17-21 F	22-26 M	22-26 F	27-31 M	27-31 F	32-36 M	32-36 F	37-41 M	37-41 F	42-46 M	42-46 F
77					100							
76					99							
75			100		98		100					
74			99		97		99					
73			98		96		98		100			
72			97		95		97		99			
71	100		95		94		96		98			
70	99		94		93		95		97			
69	97		93		92		94		96			
68	96		92		91		93		95			
67	94		91		89		92		94			
66	93		90		88		91		93		100	
65	92		89		87		90		92		99	
64	90		87		86		89		91		98	
63	89		86		85		88		90		97	
62	88		85		84		87		89		96	
61	86		84		83		86		88		94	
60	85		83		82		85		87		93	
59	83		82		81		84		86		92	
58	82		81		80		83		85		91	
57	81		79		79		82		84		90	
56	79		78		78		81		83		89	
55	78		77		77		79		82		88	
54	77		76		76		78		81		87	
53	75		75		75		77		79		86	
52	74		74		74		76		78		84	
51	72		73		73		75		77		83	
50	71		71		72	100	74		76		82	
49	70		70		71	99	73		75		81	
48	68		69		69	98	72		74		80	
47	67		68		68	96	71		73		79	
46	66		67	100	67	95	70		72		78	
45	64		66	99	66	94	69	100	71		77	
44	63		65	97	65	93	68	99	70		76	
43	61		63	96	64	92	67	97	69		74	
42	60	100	62	94	63	90	66	96	68		73	

	Table 15. Army Push-Up Standard*										
AGE GROUP	**17-21**		**22-26**		**27-31**		**32-36**		**37-41**		**42-46**	
Repetitions	M	F	M	F	M	F	M	F	M	F	M	F
41	59	98	61	93	62	89	65	95	67		72	
40	57	97	60	92	61	88	64	93	66	100	71	
39	56	95	59	90	60	87	63	92	65	99	70	
38	54	93	58	89	59	85	62	91	64	97	69	
37	53	91	57	88	58	84	61	89	63	96	68	100
36	52	90	55	86	57	83	60	88	62	94	67	98
35	50	88	54	85	56	82	59	87	61	93	66	97
34	49	86	53	83	55	81	58	85	60	91	64	95
33	48	84	52	82	54	79	57	84	59	90	63	94
32	46	83	51	81	53	78	56	83	58	88	62	92
31	45	81	50	79	52	77	55	81	57	87	61	90
30	43	79	49	78	50	76	54	80	56	85	60	89
29	42	77	47	77	49	75	53	79	55	84	59	87
28	41	76	46	75	48	73	52	77	54	82	58	86
27	39	74	45	74	47	72	51	76	53	81	57	84
26	38	72	44	72	46	71	50	75	52	79	56	82
25	37	70	43	71	45	70	49	73	51	78	54	81
24	35	69	42	70	44	68	48	72	50	76	53	79
23	34	67	41	68	43	67	47	71	49	75	52	78
22	32	65	39	67	42	66	46	69	48	73	51	76
21	31	63	38	66	41	65	45	68	47	72	50	74
20	30	62	37	64	40	64	44	67	46	70	49	73
19	28	60	36	63	39	62	43	65	45	69	48	71
18	27	58	35	61	38	61	42	64	44	67	47	70
17	26	57	34	60	37	60	41	63	43	66	46	68
16	24	55	33	59	36	59	39	61	42	64	44	66
15	23	53	31	57	35	58	38	60	41	63	43	65
14	21	51	30	56	34	56	37	59	39	61	42	63
13	20	50	29	54	33	55	36	58	38	60	41	62
12	19	48	28	52	32	54	35	56	37	59	40	60
11	17	46	27	50	31	52	34	54	36	57	39	58
10	16	44	26	49	29	50	33	52	35	56	38	57
9	14	43	25	49	28	49	32	50	34	54	37	55
8	13	41	23	48	27	49	31	49	33	53	36	54
7	12	39	22	46	26	48	30	49	32	51	34	52
6	10	37	21	45	25	47	29	48	31	50	33	50
5	9	36	20	43	24	45	28	47	30	48	32	49

Table 16. Army Sit-Up Standard*						
AGE GROUP	17-21	22-26	27-31	32-36	37-41	42-46
Repetitions	M/F	M/F	M/F	M/F	M/F	M/F
82			100			
81			99			
80		100	98			
79		99	97			
78	100	97	96			
77	98	96	95			
76	97	95	94	100	100	
75	95	93	92	99	99	
74	94	92	91	98	98	
73	92	91	90	96	97	
72	90	89	89	95	96	100
71	89	88	88	94	95	99
70	87	87	87	93	94	98
69	86	85	86	92	93	97
68	84	84	85	91	92	96
67	82	83	84	89	91	95
66	81	81	83	88	89	94
65	79	80	82	87	88	93
64	78	79	81	86	87	92
63	76	77	79	85	86	91
62	74	76	78	84	85	90
61	73	75	77	82	84	89
60	71	73	76	81	83	88
59	70	72	75	80	82	87
58	68	71	74	79	81	86
57	66	69	73	78	80	85
56	65	68	72	76	79	84
55	63	67	71	75	78	83
54	62	65	70	74	77	82
53	60	64	69	73	76	81
52	58	63	68	72	75	80
51	57	61	66	71	74	79
50	55	60	65	69	73	78
49	54	59	64	68	72	77
48	52	57	63	67	71	76
47	50	56	62	66	69	75
46	49	55	61	65	68	74
45	47	53	60	64	67	73
44	46	52	59	62	66	72

Table 16. Army Sit-Up Standard*						
AGE GROUP	17-21	22-26	27-31	32-36	37-41	42-46
Repetitions	M/F	M/F	M/F	M/F	M/F	M/F
43	44	50	58	61	65	71
42	42	49	57	60	64	70
41	41	48	56	59	63	69
40	39	47	55	58	62	68
39	38	45	54	56	61	67
38	36	44	52	55	60	66
37	34	43	51	54	59	65
36	33	41	50	53	58	64
35	31	40	49	52	57	63
34	30	39	48	50	56	62
33	28	37	47	49	55	61
32	26	36	46	48	54	60
31	25	35	45	47	53	59
30	23	33	44	46	52	58
29	22	32	43	45	50	57
28	20	31	42	44	49	56
27	18	29	41	42	48	55
26	17	28	39	41	47	54
25	15	27	38	40	46	53
24	14	25	37	39	45	52
23	12	24	36	38	44	51
22	10	23	35	36	43	50
21	9	21	34	35	42	49

AGE GROUP	17-21		22-26		27-31		32-36		37-41	
Time	M	F	M	F	M	F	M	F	M	F
12:54										
13:00	100		100							
13:06	99		99							
13:12	97		98							
13:18	96		97		100		100			
13:24	94		96		99		99			
13:30	93		94		98		98			
13:36	92		93		97		97		100	
13:42	90		92		96		96		99	
13:48	89		91		95		95		98	
13:54	88		90		94		95		97	
14:00	86		89		92		94		97	
14:06	85		88		91		93		96	
14:12	83		87		90		92		95	
14:18	82		86		89		91		94	
14:24	81		84		88		90		93	
14:30	79		83		87		89		92	
14:36	78		82		86		88		91	
14:42	77		81		85		87		91	
14:48	75		80		84		86		90	
14:54	74		79		83		85		89	
15:00	72		78		82		85		88	
15:06	71		77		81		84		87	
15:12	70		76		79		83		86	
15:18	68		74		78		82		86	
15:24	67		73		77		81		85	
15:30	66		72		76		80		84	
15:36	64	100	71	100	75		79		83	
15:42	63	99	70	99	74		78		82	
15:48	61	98	69	98	73	100	77		81	
15:54	60	96	68	97	72	99	76	100	80	
16:00	59	95	67	96	71	98	75	99	80	
16:06	57	94	66	95	70	97	75	99	79	
16:12	56	93	64	94	69	97	74	98	78	
16:18	54	92	63	93	68	96	73	97	77	
16:24	53	90	62	92	66	95	72	97	76	
16:30	52	89	61	91	65	94	71	96	75	

Table 17. Army 2-mile Run Standard*

Table 17. Army 2-mile Run Standard*									
AGE GROUP	17-21		22-26		27-31		32-36		37-41	
Time	M	F	M	F	M	F	M	F	M	F
16:36	50	88	60	90	64	93	70	95	74	
16:42	49	87	59	89	63	92	69	94	74	
16:48	48	85	58	88	62	91	68	94	73	
16:54	46	84	57	87	61	91	67	93	72	
17:00	45	83	56	86	60	90	66	92	71	100
17:06	43	82	54	85	59	89	65	92	70	99
17:12	42	81	53	84	58	88	65	91	69	99
17:18	41	79	52	83	57	87	64	90	69	98
17:24	39	78	51	82	56	86	63	90	68	97
17:30	38	77	50	81	55	86	62	89	67	96
17:36	37	76	49	80	54	85	61	88	66	96
17:42	35	75	48	79	52	84	60	88	65	95
17:48	34	73	47	78	51	83	59	87	64	94
17:54	32	72	46	77	50	82	58	86	63	94
18:00	31	71	44	76	49	81	57	86	63	93
18:06	30	70	43	75	48	80	56	85	62	92
18:12	28	68	42	74	47	80	55	84	61	92
18:18	27	67	41	73	46	79	55	83	60	91
18:24	26	66	40	72	45	78	54	83	59	90
18:30	24	65	39	71	44	77	53	82	58	89
18:36	23	64	38	70	43	76	52	81	57	89
18:42	21	62	37	69	42	75	51	81	57	88
18:48	20	61	36	68	41	74	50	80	56	87
18:54	19	60	34	67	39	74	49	79	55	87
19:00	17	59	33	66	38	73	48	79	54	86
19:06	16	58	32	65	37	72	47	78	53	85
19:12	14	56	31	64	36	71	46	77	52	85
19:18	13	55	30	63	35	70	45	77	51	84
19:24	12	54	29	62	34	69	45	76	51	83
19:30	10	53	28	61	33	69	44	75	50	82
19:36	9	52	27	60	32	68	43	74	49	82
19:42	8	50	26	59	31	67	42	74	48	81
19:48	6	49	24	58	30	66	41	73	47	80
19:54	5	48	23	57	29	65	40	72	46	80
20:00	3	47	22	56	28	64	39	72	46	79
20:06	2	45	21	55	26	63	38	71	45	78
20:12	1	44	20	54	25	63	37	70	44	78

Table 17. Army 2-mile Run Standard*										
AGE GROUP	**17-21**		**22-26**		**27-31**		**32-36**		**37-41**	
Time	M	F	M	F	M	F	M	F	M	F
20:18	0	43	19	53	24	62	36	70	43	77
20:24		42	18	52	23	61	35	69	42	76
20:30		41	17	51	22	60	35	68	41	75
20:36		39	16	50	21	59	34	68	40	75
20:42		38	14	49	20	58	33	67	40	74
20:48		37	13	48	19	57	32	66	39	73
20:54		36	12	47	18	57	31	66	38	73
21:00		35	11	46	17	56	30	65	37	72
21:06		33	10	45	16	55	29	64	36	71
21:12		32	9	44	15	54	28	63	35	71
21:18		31	8	43	14	53	27	63	34	70
21:24		30	7	42	12	52	26	62	34	69
21:30		28	6	41	11	51	25	61	33	68
21:36		27	4	40	10	51	25	61	32	68
21:42		26	3	39	9	50	24	60	31	67
21:48		25	2	38	8	49	23	59	30	66
21:54		24	1	37	7	48	22	59	29	66
22:00		22	0	36	6	47	21	58	29	65
22:06		21		35	5	46	20	57	28	64
22:12		20		34	4	46	19	57	27	64
22:18		19		33	3	45	18	56	26	63
22:24		18		32	2	44	17	55	25	62
22:30		16		31	1	43	16	54	24	61
22:36		15		30	0	42	15	54	23	61
22:42		14		29		41	15	53	23	60
22:48		13		28		40	14	52	22	59
22:54		12		27		40	13	52	21	59
23:00		10		26		39	12	51	20	58
23:06		9		25		38	11	50	19	57
23:12		8		24		37	10	49	18	56
23:18		7		23		36	9	49	17	56
23:24		5		22		35	8	48	17	55
23:30		4		21		34	7	48	16	54
23:36		3		20		34	6	47	15	54
23:42		2		19		33	5	46	14	53
23:48		1		18		32	5	46	13	52
23:54		0		17		31	4	45	12	52

Table 17. Army 2-mile Run Standard*										
AGE GROUP	17-21		22-26		27-31		32-36		37-41	
Time	M	F	M	F	M	F	M	F	M	F
24:00				16		30	3	44	11	51
24:06				15		29	2	43	11	50
24:12				14		29	1	43	10	49
24:18				13		28	0	42	9	49
24:24				12		27		41	8	48
24:30				11		26		41	7	47
24:36				10		25		40	6	47
24:42				9		24		39	6	46
24:48				8		23		39	5	45
24:54				7		23		38	4	45
25:00				6		22		37	3	44
25:06				5		21		37	2	43
25:12				4		20		36	1	42
25:18				3		19		35	0	42
25:24				2		18		34		41
25:30				1		17		34		40
25:36				0		17		33		40
25:42						16		32		39
25:48						15		32		38
25:54						14		31		38
26:00						13		30		37
26:06						12		30		36
26:12						11		29		35
26:18						11		28		35
26:24						10		28		34
26:30						9		27		33

Appendix 3

Navy Fitness Charts

How to Read the Navy Physical Fitness Charts

This scoring system assigns points based on performance categories and levels. Scores are averaged to determine the sailor's overall Physical Readiness Test (PRT) performance.

To best understand how to read the Navy fitness charts (Tables 18-24), let's use the following example: A 25-year-old female does 91 curl ups (i.e. sit-ups), which is in the category of excellent and a level of high (see Table 23). By looking at the corresponding number in the points column, you can see this female earned 85 points. This female also performed 26 push-ups, which is in the category of good and a level of medium. As you can see, she earned 65 points on her push-up test. She completed her 1.5-mile run in 15:23, which is in the category of satisfactory and the level of high. She earned 55 points on her 1.5-mile run test.

To compute an overall score, you will add the individual points (85+65+55). In this example, the total points equal 205. Next, you divide the 205 points by 3, which equals 68. By referring to Table 24 you can find her total of 68 points equals a category of good and a level of medium. You can not round up on these charts. Should this person's score have been a 70, she would have advanced to the next category and level.

You must perform all three events (push-ups, curl-ups, and a cardiovascular event) to obtain a score. To graduate boot camp, a sailor needs an average of 60 points or more in all three events.

Table 18. Navy Fitness Standards-Male, Age 17 to 19

Performance Category	Level	Points	Curl-Ups	Push-Ups	1.5 Mile Run	500 Yd Swim	450 M Swim
Outstanding	High	100	109	92	8:15	6:30	6:20
Outstanding	Medium	95	107	91	8:45	6:45	6:35
Outstanding	Low	90	102	86	9:00	7:15	7:05
Excellent	High	85	98	82	9:15	7:45	7:35
Excellent	Medium	80	93	79	9:30	8:15	8:05
Excellent	Low	75	90	76	9:45	8:30	8:20
Good	High	70	81	68	10:00	9:15	9:05
Good	Medium	65	71	60	10:30	10:30	10:20
Good	Low	60	62	51	11:00	11:15	11:05
Satisfactory	High	55	59	49	12:00	11:45	11:35
Satisfactory	Medium	50	54	46	12:15	12:15	12:05
Probationary		45	50	42	12:30	12:45	12:35

Table 19. Navy Fitness Standards-Male, Age 20 to 24

Performance Category	Level	Points	Curl-Ups	Push-Ups	1.5 Mile Run	500 Yd Swim	450 M Swim
Outstanding	High	100	105	87	8:30	6:30	6:20
Outstanding	Medium	95	103	86	9:00	7:00	6:50
Outstanding	Low	90	98	81	9:15	7:30	7:20
Excellent	High	85	94	77	9:45	8:00	7:50
Excellent	Medium	80	90	74	10:00	8:15	8:05
Excellent	Low	75	87	71	10:30	8:45	8:35
Good	High	70	78	64	10:45	9:30	9:20
Good	Medium	65	66	55	11:30	10:30	10:20
Good	Low	60	58	47	12:00	11:30	11:20
Satisfactory	High	55	54	45	12:45	12:00	11:50
Satisfactory	Medium	50	50	42	13:15	12:15	12:05
Probationary		45	46	37	13:30	13:00	12:50

Table 20. Navy Fitness Standards– Male, Age 25 to 29							
Performance		**Points**	**Curl-Ups**	**Push-Ups**	**1.5 Mile Run**	**500 Yd Swim**	**450 M Swim**
Category	**Level**						
Outstanding	High	100	101	84	8:55	6:38	6:28
Outstanding	Medium	95	100	82	9:23	7:08	6:58
Outstanding	Low	90	95	77	9:38	7:38	7:28
Excellent	High	85	91	73	10:15	8:08	7:58
Excellent	Medium	80	87	69	10:30	8:23	8:13
Excellent	Low	75	84	67	10:52	8:53	8:43
Good	High	70	75	60	11:23	9:38	9:28
Good	Medium	65	62	51	12:15	10:38	10:28
Good	Low	60	54	44	12:53	11:38	11:28
Satisfactory	High	55	50	41	13:23	12:08	11:58
Satisfactory	Medium	50	47	38	13:45	12:23	12:13
Probationary		45	43	34	14:00	13:08	12:58

| Table 21. Navy Fitness Standards- Female, Age 17 to 19 | | | | | | | |
Performance Category	Level	Points	Curl-Ups	Push-Ups	1.5 Mile Run	500 Yd Swim	450 M Swim
Outstanding	High	100	109	51	9:29	6:45	6:35
Outstanding	Medium	95	107	50	11:15	7:45	7:35
Outstanding	Low	90	102	47	11:30	8:30	8:20
Excellent	High	85	98	45	11:45	9:00	8:50
Excellent	Medium	80	93	43	12:00	9:30	9:20
Excellent	Low	75	90	42	12:30	9:45	9:35
Good	High	70	81	36	12:45	10:45	10:35
Good	Medium	65	71	30	13:00	12:00	11:50
Good	Low	60	62	24	13:30	13:00	12:50
Satisfactory	High	55	59	22	14:15	13:15	13:05
Satisfactory	Medium	50	54	20	14:45	13:45	13:35
Probationary		45	50	19	15:00	14:15	14:05

Performance		Points	Curl-Ups	Push-Ups	1.5 Mile Run	500 Yd Swim	450 M Swim
Category	Level						
Outstanding	High	100	105	48	9:47	7:15	7:05
Outstanding	Medium	95	103	47	11:15	8:00	7:50
Outstanding	Low	90	98	44	11:30	8:45	8:35
Excellent	High	85	94	43	12:15	9:15	9:05
Excellent	Medium	80	90	40	12:45	9:45	9:35
Excellent	Low	75	87	39	13:15	10:00	9:50
Good	High	70	78	33	13:30	11:00	10:50
Good	Medium	65	66	28	13:45	12:15	12:05
Good	Low	60	58	21	14:15	13:15	13:05
Satisfactory	High	55	54	20	15:00	13:45	13:35
Satisfactory	Medium	50	50	17	15:15	14:00	13:50
Probationary		45	46	16	15:30	14:30	14:20

Table 22. Navy Fitness Standards-Female, Age 20 to 24

Table 23. Navy Fitness Standards- Female, Age 25-29

Performance Category	Level	Points	Curl-Ups	Push-Ups	1.5 Mile Run	500 Yd Swim	450 M Swim
Outstanding	High	100	101	46	10:17	7:23	7:13
Outstanding	Medium	95	100	45	11:30	8:15	7:58
Outstanding	Low	90	95	43	11:45	9:00	8:50
Excellent	High	85	91	41	12:30	9:30	9:20
Excellent	Medium	80	87	39	13:00	10:00	9:50
Excellent	Low	75	84	37	13:23	10:15	10:05
Good	High	70	75	30	14:00	11:15	11:05
Good	Medium	65	62	26	14:30	12:30	12:20
Good	Low	60	54	19	14:53	13:30	13:20
Satisfactory	High	55	50	18	15:23	13:53	13:43
Satisfactory	Medium	50	47	15	15:45	14:15	14:05
Probationary		45	43	13	16:08	14:45	14:35

Table 24. Overall Scoring Point Assignments-Navy		
Category	Level	Points
Outstanding	High	100
Outstanding	Medium	95
Outstanding	Low	90
Excellent	High	85
Excellent	Medium	80
Excellent	Low	75
Good	High	70
Good	Medium	65
Good	Low	60
Satisfactory	High	55
Satisfactory	Medium	50
Probationary		45

Appendix 4

Marine Fitness Charts
_____

How to Read the Marine Physical Fitness Charts

Physical fitness for the Marines (Tables 25-28) is more important than any other branch of service. Three exercises are performed for each fitness test. For the males, the exercises are pull-ups, crunches (sit-ups), and the 3-mile run. The pull-up is not a timed event. For the females, the exercises are the flex arm hang, crunches (sit-ups), and the 3-mile run.

A minimum performance in each event alone will not total the points required for a passing score. Additional points must be earned in at least one event in order to achieve a 3rd Class ranking or better per age group. Failure to meet the minimum requirements in any event constitutes a failure of the entire test, regardless of the total number of points earned for the combined three events. All values should be rounded up. For example, if you are a female and completed your run in 21:41 you would round up to the next point category, which would equal 95 points.

To receive a passing score on the fitness test, Marines must perform the minimum acceptable performance requirements shown in Table 25 for their age-group. Additionally, they must have enough overall points to meet the 3rd class fitness requirements shown in Table 26.

Table 25. Minimum Fitness Requirements for Each Marine PFT Event - Females

Age	Flexed-Arm Hang	Crunches	3-Mile Run
17-26	15 Seconds	50	31:00
27-39	15 Seconds	45	32:00
40-45	15 Seconds	45	33:00
46+	15 Seconds	40	36:00

Table 26. Marine PFT Classification Scores - Male and Female

Class	Age 17-26	Age 27-39	Age 40-45	Age 46+
1st	225	200	175	150
2nd	175	150	125	100
3rd	135	110	88	65

Table 27. Marine Physical Fitness Test Points – Male			
Points	Pull-Ups	Crunches	3-Mile Run
100	20	100	18:00
99		99	18:10
98		98	18:20
97		97	18:30
96		96	18:40
95	19	95	18:50
94		94	19:00
93		93	19:10
92		92	19:20
91		91	19:30
90	18	90	19:40
89		89	19:50
88		88	20:00
87		87	20:10
86		86	20:20
85	17	85	20:30
84		84	20:40
83		83	20:50
82		82	21:00
81		81	21:10
80	16	80	21:20
79		79	21:30
78		78	21:40
77		77	21:50
76		76	22:00
75	15	75	22:10
74		74	22:20
73		73	22:30
72		72	22:40

Points	Pull-Ups	Crunches	3-Mile Run
71		71	22:50
70	14	70	23:00
69		69	23:10
68		68	23:20
67		67	23:30
66		66	23:40
65	13	65	23:50
64		64	24:00
63		63	24:10
62		62	24:20
61		61	24:30
60	12	60	24:40
59		59	24:50
58		58	25:00
57		57	25:10
56		56	25:20
55	11	55	25:30
54		54	25:40
53		53	25:50
52		52	26:00
51		51	26:10
50	10	50	26:20
49		49	26:30
48		48	26:40
47		47	26: 50
46		46	27:00
45	9	45	27:10
44		44	27:20
43		43	27:30

Table 27. Marine Physical Fitness Test Points - Male

Table 27. Marine Physical Fitness Test Points – Male			
Points	Pull-Ups	Crunches	3-Mile Run
42		42	27:40
41		41	27:50
40	8	40	28:00
39		x	28:10
38		x	28:20
37		x	28:30
36		x	28:40
35	7	x	28:50
34		x	29:00
33		x	29:10
32		x	29:20
31		x	29:30
30	6	x	29:40
29		x	29:50
28		x	30:00
27		x	30:10
26		x	30:20
25	5	x	30:30
24		x	30:40
23		x	30:50
22		x	31:00
21		x	31:10
20	4	x	31:20
19		x	31:30
18		x	31:40
17		x	31:50
16		x	32:00
15	3	x	32:10
14	x	x	32:20

Table 27. Marine Physical Fitness Test Points - Male			
Points	Pull-Ups	Crunches	3-Mile Run
13	x	x	32:30
12	x	x	32:40
11	x	x	32:50
10	x	x	33:00
9	x	x	x
8	x	x	x
7	x	x	x
6	x	x	x
5	x	x	x
4	x	x	x
3	x	x	x
2	x	x	x
1	x	x	x

Points	Flexed-Arm Hang	Crunches	3-Mile Run
100	70 sec	100	21:00
99		99	21:10
98	69 sec	98	21:20
97		97	21:30
96	68 sec	96	21:40
95		95	21:50
94	67 sec	94	22:00
93		93	22:10
92	66 sec	92	22:20
91		91	22:30
90	65 sec	90	22:40
89		89	22:50
88	64 sec	88	23:00
87		87	23:10
86	63 sec	86	23:20
85		85	23:30
84	62 sec	84	23:40
83		83	23:50
82	61 sec	82	24:00
81		81	24:10
80	60 sec	80	24:20
79		79	24:30
78	59 sec	78	24:40
77		77	24:50
76	58 sec	76	25:00
75		75	25:10
74	57 sec	74	25:20
73		73	25:30
72	56 sec	72	25:40

Table 28. Marine Physical Fitness Test Points - Female

Table 28. Marine Physical Fitness Test Points - Female			
Points	Flexed-Arm Hang	Crunches	3-Mile Run
71		71	25:50
70	55 sec	70	26:00
69		69	26:10
68	54 sec	68	26:20
67		67	26:30
66	53 sec	66	26:40
65		65	26: 50
64	52 sec	64	27:00
63		63	27:10
62	51 sec	62	27:20
61		61	27:30
60	50 sec	60	27:40
59		59	27:50
58	49 sec	58	28:00
57		57	28:10
56	48 sec	56	28:20
55		55	28:30
54	47 sec	54	28:40
53		53	28:50
52	46 sec	52	29:00
51		51	29:10
50	45 sec	50	29:20
49		49	29:30
48	44 sec	48	29:40
47		47	29:50
46	43 sec	46	30:00
45		45	30:10
44	42 sec	44	30:20
43		43	30:30

Points	Flexed-Arm Hang	Crunches	3-Mile Run
\multicolumn{4}{l}{Table 28. Marine Physical Fitness Test Points – Female}			
42	41 sec	42	30:40
41		41	30:50
40	40 sec	40	31:00
39	39 sec	x	31:10
38	38 sec	x	31:20
37	37 sec	x	31:30
36	36 sec	x	31:40
35	35 sec	x	31:50
34	34 sec	x	32:00
33	33 sec	x	32:10
32	32 sec	x	32:20
31	31 sec	x	32:30
30	30 sec	x	32:40
29	29 sec	x	32:50
28	28 sec	x	33:00
27	27 sec	x	33:10
26	26 sec	x	33:20
25	25 sec	x	33:30
24	24 sec	x	33:40
23	23 sec	x	33:50
22	22 sec	x	34:00
21	21 sec	x	34:10
20	20 sec	x	34:20
19	19 sec	x	34:30
18	18 sec	x	34:40
17	17 sec	x	34:50
16	16 sec	x	35:00
15	15 sec	x	35:10
14	x	x	35:20

Table 28. Marine Physical Fitness Test Points - Female			
Points	Flexed-Arm Hang	Crunches	3-Mile Run
13	x	x	35:30
12	x	x	35:40
11	x	x	35:50
10	x	x	36:00
9	x	x	x
8	x	x	x
7	x	x	x
6	x	x	x
5	x	x	x
4	x	x	x
3	x	x	x
2	x	x	x
1	x	x	x

Appendix 5

Air Force Fitness Charts

How to Read the Air Force Physical Fitness Charts

Fitness in the Air Force is a bit different than the other branches, so it is important that you read this carefully and do not simply rely upon other charts and requirements for different branches of the service.

Instead of categorizing fitness standards based on age, you are categorized by your gender. To graduate from Air Force Basic Training, you must be able to perform the following minimum standards:

Males:

Two Mile Run: 16:45
1.5 Mile Run: 11:57
Sit-Ups: 50 (in 2 minutes)
Push-Ups: 45 (in 2 minutes)

Females:

Two Mile Run: 19:45
1.5 Mile Run: 13:56

Sit-Ups: 50 (in 2 minutes)
Push-Ups: 27 (in 2 minutes)

Recruits could be awarded the "Warhawk" Physical Fitness Award for achieving outstanding levels of physical fitness. Those who qualify for the Warhawk Physical Fitness Award receive (among other things) an extra town pass on graduation weekend. By receiving a town pass, you will get to go off-base on the Sunday following graduation. To qualify for the Warhawk Physical Fitness Award, the minimum standards that must be reached are:

Males:

Two Mile Run: 13:30
1.5 mile Run: 08:08
Sit-Ups: 80 (in 2 minutes)
Push-Ups: 75 (in 2 minutes)
Pull-Ups: 10

Females:

Two Mile Run: 15:00
1.5 Mile Run: 10:55
Sit-Ups: 75 (in 2 minutes)
Push-Ups: 40 (in 2 minutes)
Pull-Ups: 5

Appendix 6

Coast Guard Fitness Charts

How to Read the Coast Guard Physical Fitness Charts

Fitness in the Coast Guard is a bit different than it is in the other branches, so it is important that you read this carefully and do not simply rely upon other charts and requirements for different branches of the service.

Instead of categorizing fitness standards based on age, you are categorized by your gender. To graduate from Coast Guard Basic Training, you must be able to perform the following minimum standards:

Males:

1.5 Mile Run: 12:51
Sit-Ups: 38 (in 60 seconds)
Push-Ups: 29 (in 60 seconds)

Females:

1.5 Mile Run: 15:26
Sit-Ups: 32 (in 60 seconds)
Push-Ups: 23 (in 60 seconds)

In addition to the above standards you will also have a swimming test. The minimum standards of the swimming test are as follows:

Swimming Test:

Tread water 5 minutes
Jump off 5-foot platform into a pool and swim 100 meters.

Answer Key

Below, broken into chapter sections, are the answers to the questions found in this workbook. It is important that you read the answer carefully, re-read the question, and then think about it for a few moments before moving on.

This is also a good time to remind you that this is an <u>interactive</u> workbook. As I earlier wrote, throughout this book, icons have been inserted next to specific questions. Whenever you spot one, open your Internet browser and click over to www.ultimatebasictraining.com/interactive, where you can view the interactive answers to the questions associated with these icons. I have tried to do everything I can to make this workbook a rich and helpful primer to help you prepare for basic training and your career in the military.

<u>Don't skip the online answers</u>! <u>They are important</u>!

*   *   *

Chapter 1: Multiple Choice Answers

1. C. Your shoelace.

A "snake" is a portion of your shoelace that sticks out of your boot. In basic training you must have all your shoelaces tucked into your boot.

2. D. 40%.

Unrealistic expectations? There are several reasons why recruits don't make it, but the correct answer to this question is 40%. Forty percent of soldiers fail to surpass their 4th year in the military.

3. D. 0

Use of tobacco products are strictly prohibited during basic training.

4. B. Your bed/bunk.

A hospital corner is a special way to make your bed. You should know how to do a hospital corner before you arrive for basic training.

5. A. Romeo.

Never go to basic training without knowing the phonetic alphabet, backward and forward, in advance!

6. B. Never eat dessert.

Unless you like pushups, don't eat dessert during basic training. If you selected letter "D" for this answer, give yourself 100 push ups.

7. D. Never.

Don't even bother bringing your contact lenses with you to basic training, they are not allowed. You will be issued military glasses, and believe me, you will be looking good in those glasses!

8. B. A series of field equipment inspected often by Drill Sergeants.

You will be issued field equipment upon arriving at boot camp. This equipment is known as TA-50. Before you graduate you must know how to clean this equipment to a condition better than you received it in.

9. D. Never sneeze in formation.

Do not move for any reason while at the position of attention, and shouting something after you do so will only get you into trouble more.

10. B. Meals, Ready-to-Eat.

11. D. 100 months.

The shelf life of a typical MRE stored at a constant 70 degrees F is 100 months.

12. B. Pouch bread.

MRE bread is called "pouch bread" because it comes sealed in what's called a protective tri-laminate pouch.

13. C. Hot sauce.

Soldiers like the option of hot sauce regardless of what they are eating.

14. C. 1980s.

They replaced C-rations in the early 1980s.

15. D. 1,200 calories.

Each M.R.E provides approximately 1200 calories.

16. C. 1,250 feet.

MREs must be capable of withstanding parachute drops from 1250 feet, and non-parachute drops of 100 feet.

17. D. $7.25.

Each M.R.E costs the government approximately $7.25. The cost of a 12 pack case of MREs is $86.98.

18. A. campaign.

The distinct round hats drill sergeants wear are called campaign hats.

19. C. Anti-tank missile.

With a maximum range of 2,100 meters, the 4 pound, 40-inch right shoulder fired AT-4 (anti-tank missile) is effective when attacking enemy personnel and equipment.

20. B. Back-blast area all clear!

The black-blast area is 65 meters in a 90-degree fan behind the weapon. Make sure the area is clear before firing the weapon.

21. C. From as far as possible behind your fighting position.

To prevent the enemy from noticing where the foliage was taken, acquire the foliage from as far as possible behind your fighting position. Never use mud, it will crack, flake, and fade as it dries.

22. D. TRICARE.

TRICARE is the Department of Defense's health care program

23. A. 02 Apr. 06.

Military dates should be written from smallest to biggest units: day, month and year. The military limits the number of letters used to abbreviate the month to 3.

24. A. "O two hundred hours, Drill Sergeant!"

If you answered "D," return to page 1 of this book and start all over again.

25. B. A cadence.

There are hundreds of cadences you can sing while marching and running in the military. Remember, the beat is on the left foot.

26. A. M16/A2.

At basic training, you will be issued an M16/A2. To avoid having to do push ups, always point your rifle down range and never refer to your rifle as a "gun."

27. D. Index locking.

The four fundamentals of marksmanship are: steady position, proper aim, breathing, and trigger squeeze.

28. B. SPORTS

Slap, pull, observe, release, tap, shoot (or squeeze). This is a quick fix method if your rifle doesn't fire properly. You will learn the details at basic training.

29. C. 7.78 pounds.

A standard M16/A2 rifle without a magazine or sling weights 7.78 pounds.

30. B. 3,600 meters.

The maximum range is 3,600 meters and the maximum effective range for a point target is 550 meters.

31. C. 30 rounds.

A round is also known as a bullet and the M-16/A2 rifle holds 30 rounds in a single magazine.

32. D. 39 5/8 inches.

The length of a standard M16/A2 rifle is 39 5/8 inches.

33. D. You should never try to make friends with your Drill Sergeant.

Drill sergeants are not your friends. Their job is to break you down as a civilian and build you back up into a soldier in a short amount of time; there is no time for making friends.

34. B. 1949.

The Geneva Conventions, along with 3 other international agreements, were written on August 12, 1949.

35. D. All of the above.

The only information you are required to give as a POW is your name, age, rank and service number.

36. C. Whether the recipient is an officer or enlisted.

Whether the recipient is an officer or enlisted, that soldier is entitled to a salute.

37. C. Every 24 hours.

In basic training, you will learn about challenge and passwords which are used to identify unknown personnel at a security checkpoint. Challenge and passwords should be changed every 24 hours.

38. C. Marines.

Although the Air Force has a much bigger budget, the Marines have a resounding capability to turn their budget into firepower.

39. C. Marines.

Marines are sometimes referred to as Jarheads. There are many debates as to the origin of the term.

40. A. Speak softly.

Be confident with your answers and respond loudly and correctly to a Drill Sergeant. Speaking softly does not emphasize a person's strength, confidence, or pride.

41. D. Basic training is 95% mental and 5% physical.

By understanding what is expected of you mentally and preparing accordingly, the physical aspect of basic training accounts for only a small percentage of the overall difficulty of basic training.

42. C. To break a recruit down as a civilian and build a recruit up into a soldier.

Although the other answers of this question may be true, the drill sergeants' main goal is to break you down as a civilian and build you up into a soldier.

43. A. With small talk.

Approaching a recruit with small talk is a great way to make friends early, and you can never have enough friends during basic training. Offering to help shine their boots will make you seem like a pushover. By telling them you had a friend or relative attend basic training they will expect you know all the answers; and when they find out you don't, you will not be respected. To approach a recruit with small talk, ask them where they are from. You will be with recruits from all over the country and they most certainly will want to talk about home.

44. B. I love my country.

Whether or not the other statements are true, you would not have joined the military if you did not love your country. A drill sergeant doesn't want to hear that you needed a job; they understand that love of country is the best and most motivational reason for joining the military. By giving this answer, you might find a connection with your drill sergeant too. Becoming a drill sergeant is not easy and they definitely *must* love their country to do what they do.

45. A. Early morning.

Performing your workout routine during the early morning will best prepare you for your early morning workouts in the military.

46. B. To anticipate jet lag.

If you are in a different time zone than where you will attend basic training, it is a great idea to adjust your sleeping schedule before you arrive. This way, you wont experience jet lag and you will maximize the time you get to sleep at basic training.

47. D. Don't snack at any time, period.

There is no snacking at basic training.

48. D. Zero.

There is no smoking at basic training. If you smoke or are addicted to any kind of tobacco products, do yourself a favor and quit <u>before</u> you arrive at basic training. It is better to quit on your own terms than on your drill sergeants terms.

49. C. A permit to enter or leave a military installation for a given period of time.

You might be offered a pass at basic training, but be aware, you're more than likely to get them taken away than you will use them. Often, drill sergeants like to tempt you with a pass, and then take them away to break your spirits. A great tip for you is to not expect anything at basic training unless you actually get it.

50. B. Designer luggage.

You are asking for trouble if you arrive at basic training with luggage decorated with flowers or fancy designs. You will stick out like a sore thumb, and I can guarantee you the drill sergeants will give you a "special" welcome.

51. A. Your first day.

Your most memorable day at basic training will most likely be your first day of basic training. Otherwise known as "Day 1," this is the first time you will feel the experience of being at basic training and undoubtedly it will feel like 3 days in 1.

52. B. Rice.

If possible, eat every meal with rice. Not only is rice good for you, it expands in your stomach giving you that full feeling. Feeling full at basic training is important since you have to eat so fast and do without snacking.

53. D. Make a sandwich out of everything.

The fastest way to eat your meals at basic training is to make a sandwich out of everything. Take a piece of bread, slap some mash potatoes on that bread, mix in peas and macaroni, and you're eating almost your entire meal in no time. It might sound bad to eat, but it all goes to the same place anyway.

54. D. All of the above.

If you have time to eat a dessert at basic training, you have time to fill your stomach with protein and carbohydrates. Your body will need fuel, feed it right.

55. D. None of the above.

Adding condiments to your food will take valuable time away from eating your meals. In basic training you only have a few minutes to eat an entire meal, don't waste time shaking salt and pepper on your food. Remember, in basic training you are not there to taste your food—you are there to eat it!

56. A. 15 seconds.

Anyone who has been through basic training before can tell you that when a drill sergeant says to be somewhere in a certain amount of time, always arrive early.

57. C. Quick tie laces.

Your military boots come equipped with what's called quick tie laces. Quick tie laces allow you to lace your boots fast, so you won't be late for formation.

58. B. Hospital corner.

Every morning you will be required to make your bunk and use hospital corners. Practice on your own bed before you arrive at basic training and you will be one step ahead of every other recruit.

59. D. Hotel Juliet.

You will learn the phonetic alphabet by heart in basic training. The phonetic alphabet is useful for many reasons. One of the main reasons is so one soldier does not misinterpret another soldier's transmission. A misinterpreted grid coordinate when reading a map could mean the difference between life and death.

60. C. Assign someone you trust specific power of attorney.

There are two types of power of attorney. General power of attorney grants someone significant power. A specific power of attorney might be the route to take if you want someone to handle only specific portions of your financial or personal obligations.

61. A. One.

Try to limit yourself to only one suitcase or duffle bag.

62. D. Non-prescription drugs.

You will not be allowed to consume non-prescription drugs during basic training. If you get sick, you will be sent to the doctor and they will prescribe you medication.

63. C. They are only allowed with a doctor's note.

Unless you have a doctor's note, you can not use prescription drugs at basic training; this includes birth control pills.

64. D. Never.

Never remove food from the chow hall. Every cycle someone gets caught stealing crackers or some other small item. Do not be the recruit who does this!

65. C. You are giving up.

Showing your palm while you salute signifies you are giving up. Practice your salute before you arrive at basic training.

66. D. All of your items.

Put your initials on absolutely all of your personal gear. This includes underwear, toothbrush, shaving cream, etc. You don't want to be the one with missing underwear (and yes, it does happen).

67. C. Buy ones where the pre-recorded message doesn't talk too much.

You only get a few minutes of phone time at basic training. You don't want that phone time wasted by a prerecorded message of an operator talking at half speed. Test out some phone cards before you leave, and see which one will connect you the fastest.

68. D. Always carry one in your pocket.

You never know when a Drill Sergeant is going to tell you that you missed a spot shaving. If s/he does, you better have a tool handy to correct it on the spot. I suggest carrying a travel razor which has the shaving cream in the handle. It is never fun to shave dry.

69. B. Get it cut by a professional before you leave for basic training.

The military doesn't put much care into their haircuts. Women should get their hair cut, by a professional, to extend no longer than the bottom edge of their collar.

70. D. Never.

Drill sergeants are not authorized to strike recruits.

71. D. Any or all of the above.

The controversial, yet widely used, term has no specific origin. There is much debate as to the origin, but the definition can fit choice A, B, or C.

72. B. 10-15%.

About 10-15% of recruits who start basic training will not graduate.

73. D. It is extremely difficult to get honorably discharged.

When you joined the military, you made an oath to your country and signed a contract. Because of this, it is extremely difficult to get an honorable discharge (you don't want a dishonorable one!). If you don't like basic training, it is easier to continue on and count your days rather than try and get honorably discharged.

74. A. Approximately 1/2 mile.

In military terms, a "klick" means a distance of 1000 meters (one kilometer, or .62 miles).

75. B. Vacation or liberty.

Sorry, you will not get "leave" at basic training.

76. B. A duty (often at night) that requires a recruit take head count, guard other soldiers, and perform chores upon the Drill Sergeant's discretion.

You and your fellow recruits will rotate fireguard shifts at basic training. Often, they last about an hour. During that hour you might be asked to do chores for a Drill Sergeant, take head count, or simply stay awake and make sure nothing out of the ordinary occurs.

77. B. In the kitchen.

KP is an acronym short for kitchen patrol.

78. C. Laws and regulations encompassing the military.

UCMJ stands for the Uniform Code of Military Justice. The UCMJ was enacted by Congress in 1950 (and went into effect the following year) to establish a standard set of criminal laws for all the U.S. military services.

79. D. "This we'll defend."

The next time you see an Army Drill Sergeant, look at his/her patch. You will notice the phrase "this we'll defend"; don't stare too long, though! You don't want any added attention.

80. B. A military test.

The ASVAB is an acronym for the Armed Services Vocational Aptitude Battery. The ASVAB is a test given by the United States Armed Services and it measures a recruit's aptitude. Based on the results of this test, a recruit will have a better idea of what military job they are best suited for.

81. D. Get sick.

Don't be surprised when you get to basic training if you come down with a cold. With all the physical and mental stress you are putting on your body, coupled with dirty hands and being so close to many fellow recruits, getting sick is inevitable.

82. D. Marines.

Physically and mentally, Marines have the most difficult basic training of all the branches.

83. A. Nothing different.

A common question females have is: What do I do during my "time of the month"? Pads and tampons are available for use and bathroom breaks are given often enough that changing pads and tampons are not a problem. In fact, many women report they don't even have a cycle during basic training due to the high levels of stress.

84. C. Water.

Simple H_2O is used to create an exothermic reaction and heat the food in an MRE.

85. B. You will have to do an intense physical workout as punishment for an infraction.

Don't get your hopes up; everyone will get "smoked" in basic training at least once, even if you're perfect. You might even get smoked for being perfect.

86. A. Secure your wall locker.

Always make sure your wall locker is secure, even if you walk away from it for just 20 seconds.

87. D. A section of the UCMJ that provides for swift non-judicial punishment for minor offenses.

If you misbehave at basic training, your Drill Sergeants might threaten you with an Article 15. If you receive an Article 15 you could lose rank and pay.

88. D. More than 75.

About 80% of all jobs in the military are non-combat occupations.

89. C. Preparatory command.

The preparatory command states the movement to be carried out and mentally prepares the soldier for its execution.

90. A. Command of execution.

The command of execution tells the soldier when the movement is to be carried out.

91. D. Treaties that set the standards for international law for humanitarian concerns.

The Geneva Conventions consist of treaties formulated in Geneva, Switzerland that set the standards for international law for humanitarian concerns.

92. C. Geneva, Switzerland.

93. C. The varying pitch of the voice of an individual giving commands.

At basic training, you will learn how to present inflection when giving marching commands.

94. A. "As you were!"

Saying "as you were" strikes the previous command given in formation.

95. B. Purity and innocence.

Regarding the American flag, the color red represents blood, hardiness and valor; the color white represents purity and innocence; and the color blue represents honor for vigilance, perseverance and justice.

96. D. A company, battery, or troop identification flag.

The guidon is a company, battery, or troop identification flag. It is present at all unit formations unless otherwise directed by the commander.

97. D. Every soldier.

Every soldier should carry a first aid pack in combat.

98. C. CPR.

CPR is a technique designed to circulate blood through the body of a person whose heart has stopped, not to clear an obstruction in one's throat.

99. B. Bone.

There are two types of fractures: compound or open fracture (bone protruding through the skin) and simple or closed fracture (bone not protruding through the skin).

100. C. Man-made objects.

On a military map, blue represents water, green represents vegetation, red-brown represents cultural features and elevation, red represents main roads and populated areas, black represents man-made objects and brown represents relief features.

101. A. High.

The three types of north you may find on a military map are true, magnetic, and north.

102. B. We will never use them.

The United States has adopted the following policy toward Nuclear Biological and Chemical (NBC) Warfare: nuclear: we will use first if need be (first strike), biological: we will never use, chemical: we will use them only after enemy uses them first.

103. C. Paper.

Paint, earth, sand, clay, and gravel are just a few materials you can use to camouflage shiny areas on equipment to avoid detection.

104. C. A rally point is an area where soldiers convene.

A leader among a group of soldiers might designate a rally point before or during an exercise or operation.

105. C. Water.

The military recognizes water as the most important need in a survival situation.

106. C. On a soldier's body.

A BDU stands for Battle Dress Uniform.

107. D. Sergeants.

Generally, an officer plans and coordinates the details of a mission and the sergeants carry out the details, thus, usually referred to as the backbone of the military.

108. C. You get to basic training.

Generally, your friends and family will not know where to write you until you get to basic training. As soon as you get your address, write a letter to your friends and family.

109. C. Pass a rigorous and stressful course.

Each branch of service is different regarding the training of Drill Sergeants, but overall you can bet your Drill Sergeant is prepared to turn you into a soldier.

110. C. In the past, new recruits were called "boots."

It's true. Drill Sergeants used to call recruits "boots," hence the term *boot camp*, which remains a common phrase today.

111. B. Recycled.

Don't misbehave, or you might get recycled.

112. A. To greet with an expression of welcome or respect.

When you salute another soldier, you are greeting that soldier with an expression of welcome or respect.

113. B. 45 .

When standing at the position of attention, your feet should be 45 degrees apart.

114. C. Marines.

The Marines are the only branch of service that requires pull ups to pass the fitness tests.

Chapter 2: True or False answers

1. True. Direct deposit is mandatory for military pay at basic training. Do yourself a favor and set up a bank account before you arrive at basic training.

2. False. Your battle buddy will most likely not be the same age and race as you. Drill Sergeants prefer to pair you up with someone you don't normally socialize with on a daily basis.

3. False.

4. True. You will do a lot of running in basic training. Proper running starts by selecting the proper running shoe. You can not determine which running shoe is right for you without knowing if you have a low, normal or high arch foot, consult *The Ultimate Basic Training Guidebook* for details on how to find the proper arch type of your foot, or see Figure 1 in Chapter 8 of this book.

5. False. When stretching the quadriceps muscle, do not pull with your toe. Place your hand on your ankle and pull upward. Pulling your toes will put too much stress on your ankles and not properly stretch the quadriceps.

6. True. Before you leave for basic training, you should know the distance of your stride. By knowing your stride you can estimate how long you have run without predetermining the distance of your route first. A stride is calculated by measuring the distance of ten normal sized steps and dividing the distance you walked by ten.

7. False. A common running movement is to run heal to toe, but ideally, you want your mid-foot to touch the ground first. When you land on your heels, you are placing your body's center of gravity behind you. This forces you to push harder with every step and wastes energy.

8. True. When running, your foot should land under your body when it strikes the ground, not in front of you. By doing this, you will ensure better leverage and balance.

9. False. Do not shave your head before you leave for basic training. The military will give you hair cuts.

10. False. In basic training, there is no gym. You will be using your own body weight as resistance. Stop going to the gym and start doing compound movements (exercises that use more than one muscle group at a time). Compound movements (i.e. push ups, squats, etc) can be done at home with or without weights.

11. False. One of the best times of the day for a recruit is when the Drill Sergeant says it is time for mail call. Don't tell your friends or relatives to mail you candy or snacks. That will certainly lead to trouble. They are authorized to send you letters, photographs, and calling cards.

12. True.

13. False. Cell phones are not allowed at basic training. To call home, you most likely will use a pay phone, only when authorized by a Drill Sergeant.

14. False. Women comprise about 20% of the total population of the U.S. military. Also, the percentage of women serving on active duty in the military has more than doubled since the 1970s.

15. False. Drill Sergeants will not allow you to use an electric razor at basic training.

16. False. Please don't bring cologne or perfume with you to basic training, your only asking for trouble if you do so.

17. False. Female Drill Sergeants are no nicer or meaner than male Drill Sergeant. Each Drill Sergeant has a job to do, and that is to get you military tough in a short amount of time, that requires all Drill Sergeants, male or female, to be strict.

18. False. This is a big misconception recruits carry with them to basic training. There will always be a few recruits you meet at basic training that seem to spend their life at sick call. Believe me; they are not getting out of Drills. Every recruit has knowledge to learn and physical requirements to meet. If a recruit misses these requirements they stay longer at basic training to catch up.

19. False. Run straight in a vertical alignment. Your body should be angled forward to the point where you will almost feel like falling over. Be careful not to stick your buttocks out, it will create improper balance.

20. True. Don't bounce when you run. Use your energy to create horizontal and not vertical movement. The less vertical movement you have when running, the more energy you can use to propel your body forward.

21. False. Resist the temptation to push off with your toes. By contracting your hamstring muscles (as described in quick fix #5) you will save energy for those long runs.

22. False. Basic training is remarkably similar no matter which military basic you are assigned to attend. Although slight variations will exist, your experience will be the same no matter where you attend basic training.

23. True. Remember, in basic training you don't want to draw attention to yourself. Birthdays are a prime example. If you announce to everyone it is your birthday, you will undoubtedly get special treatment for the day from your Drill Sergeants. This special treatment might not be the type of attention you were hoping for.

Working out before breakfast allows your body to use stored fat as fuel, instead of carbohydrates. Thus, you burn more fat by working out before breakfast as apposed to after breakfast.

24. True. By working out before breakfast, your body burns fat instead of carbohydrates.

25. False. Drill Sergeants are not only soldiers; they are usually some of the finest soldiers in their branch of the military. They should be looked up to as much as feared.

26. True.

27. True. Your Drill Sergeant will not call you a soldier until you have graduated basic training. Do not make the mistake of referring to yourself as a soldier either.

28. False. Do not refer to your rifle as a gun.

29. False.

30. True. Leaning on a wall, bunk, or another recruit to show your Drill Sergeant you are tired is a bad idea. Remember, you want your Drill Sergeant to perceive you as tough, not someone who needs support.

31. False. Drinking any type of alcoholic beverage at basic training will get you in trouble. The entire purpose of basic training is for your Drill Sergeants to condition you to think that a soldier must kill the enemy to be successful.

32. False. A Drill Sergeant's job is to train recruits to work successfully in a team and be able to rely on one another no matter how tough the mission might be.

33. True. Your Drill Sergeant will be watching your body language, be sure not to slouch. If your Drill Sergeant sees you are tired, he will surely wake you up. Showing your own style of a salute is a great way to impress your Drill Sergeant.

34. False. Many recruits try to add their own style to a salute, do not do this. A salute has strict form and should not be changed based on individual preference.

35. False. Warrant officers possess a high degree of specialization in a particular field in contrast to the general commissioned officers.

36. True. It is a fact that employers love to see military experience on a resume. A normal 8 hour civilian workday does not compare to a normal day in basic training. Being able to graduate from military basic training shows your prospective employers that you are a hard worker.

37. False. Day 1 is clearly one of the worst days of basic training. Your Drill Sergeants do not want to give you the wrong impression of why you are there.

38. False. Constantly changing between walking and running will disrupt your heartbeat and other bodily rhythms. During a run, it's better to continue at a constant pace. Most of the exhaustion you feel when running is mental.

39. True. Going to church or attending other religious functions is often seen as a mental break for many recruits.

40. False. Many soldiers never see combat. Serving your country doesn't mean you have to kill enemy soldiers.

41. False. Rubbing your eyes will make the discomfort worse.

42. This answer is actually half true and half false. Military food contains minimal salt and pepper in their recipes. Do not add salt and pepper to your food, it wastes valuable eating time.

Chapter 3: What Would You Do Answers

1. If your Drill Sergeants told you not to speak to anyone, you better not speak to anyone. First and foremost, follow the instructions of your Drill Sergeants. Picture this scenario: you nudge the recruit who is falling asleep and whisper "wake up." The Drill Sergeant catches you and soon everyone is doing exercises because of you—not the recruit who was falling asleep. Although teamwork is a big part of basic training, this is a scenario that requires you to fend for yourself to avoid getting yourself (and often everyone) in trouble.

2. You should never be late for formation and you should never leave your battle buddy behind. Put it this way, if you are late for formation, you will get in trouble. Conversely, if your battle buddy is late, you will get in trouble. Either way, you are going to get in trouble. So in this scenario, help your battle buddy. At least if you help him/her, you have a chance of being on time for formation.

3. A Drill Sergeant should never physically hit you. If this happens, go to your commanding officer. Make sure your claim is valid and not exaggerated in any way.

4. While on a run with your fellow recruits, you should never walk. The repercussions of a Drill Sergeant seeing you walking are far worse than the actual run itself. Walking while you are suppose to run shows your Drill Sergeants that you are not motivated or dedicated, and those are two key aspects they look for in recruits.

5. Although honesty is your best policy, it is not wise to say, "I joined for the college money" or "I needed a steady paycheck." You joined because you love your country, whether you realize it or not. Guess what? Drill Sergeants love their

country, too. Why else would they undergo such intensive training programs to train new recruits who do nothing but make them mad for months on end? Therefore, show some commonality between you and your Drill Sergeant and tell him/her you love your country.

6. Wall lockers should always be secure in basic training. Do not lock the locker for your fellow recruit because the keys may be inside the locker. If the lock is a combination lock, then maybe that would be a possibility. The best scenario is to grab a fellow recruit to guard the locker. You would have to find the recruit in the shower and inform him/her of the situation. If s/he gives you permission to lock it, then do so. Otherwise, do not.

7. Stress levels are high at basic training and some recruits don't know how to deal with stress. This situation is more common than you may think. When this occurs, tell your Drill Sergeants immediately, because they have procedures they will follow for situations like these.

8. First impressions are important at basic training, so be sure to make a good one. However, if you don't make a good first impression, be sure to follow exactly what the Drill Sergeant says, and within a short time s/he will move on to the next recruit. Mentally, you have to remember Drill Sergeants don't personally hate you, because they do not personally know you. It is their job to make basic training as hard and tough as possible. As long as you don't take anything personally and understand "the rules of the game" (that means everything in this workbook), you should do fine.

9. Every group of recruits includes someone who thinks he or she is a leader. Knowledge doesn't produce quality leaders—results do. Therefore, you can follow his or her lead if you like, but just remember to follow the orders of the Drill Sergeants first. Drill Sergeants love to pick on recruits who *think* they are leaders.

The purpose of basic training is to break you down as a civilian and build you up into a solider. Therefore, Drill Sergeants don't like individuality. If you feel the need to model after a leader, I would look to your Drill Sergeant first and not a fellow recruit. A Drill Sergeant has become a Drill Sergeant because s/he is already a proven leader.

Chapter 4: Matching Answers

1.

Army/National Guard	B. Victory Forge
Navy	A. Battle Stations
Marines	D. Crucible
Air Force	C. Warrior Week

2.

Army/National Guard	D. Has hundreds of MOSs
Navy	B. Deep routed with traditions and customs
Marines	A. Considered rifleman first
Coast Guard	C. Has 25 enlisted jobs to choose from
Air Force	E. The most impressive compilation of technology and machinery of all the branches

3.

Army/National Guard	C. Service ribbon
Navy	A. Ball cap
Marines	B. Eagle, Globe, and Anchor
Air Force	D. Training ribbon

4.

Number of smoking breaks you get per day at basic training: D. 0

Number of suitcases you should pack for basic training: E. 1

Percentage of women in the military: C. 20

The number of degrees your feet should be spread apart at the position of attention: A. 45

Percentage of all jobs in the military that are non-combat occupations: B. 80

5.

Army/National Guard	D. HUA
Navy	B. Seaman
Marines	C. OohRah
Air Force	A. Airman

6.

0001	D. Zero zero zero one
0100	C. Zero one hundred hours
1000	B. Ten hundred hours
1100	A. Eleven hundred hours

7.

0001	C. 12:01 am
0100	B. 1:00 am
1000	A. 10:00 am
1100	D. 11:00 am

8.

Put this item on first: D. Brown t-shirt
Put this item on second: C. Socks
Put this item on third: A. Pants
Put this item on last: B. Boots

9.

Always do this: B. Drink plenty of water

If given the option, always do this: A. Choose brown rice

Never do this: C. Eat dessert

Try and do this as often as possible: D. Make a sandwich out of your meals

10.

Deep knee bends: C. Dusting your boots

Running in place, hands on the ground: D. Mountain climbers

Hopping from side to side: A. Ski jumpers

Jumping, touch your heels to buttocks: B. Donkey kicks

Chapter 5: Word Games: The Phonetic Alphabet Answers

1. BUTTON. Answer: Bravo, Uniform, Tango, Tango, Oscar, November

2. FLOWER. Answer: Foxtrot, Lima, Oscar, Whiskey, Echo, Romeo

3. PUSH. Answer: Papa, Uniform, Sierra, Hotel

4. CITY. Answer: Charlie, India, Tango, Yankee

5. ZEST. Answer: Zulu, Echo, Sierra, Tango

6. ABLE. Answer: Alpha, Bravo, Lima, Echo

7. JAVA. Answer: Juliet, Alpha, Victor, Alpha

8. GIRL. Answer: Golf, India, Romeo, Lima

9. QUAIL. Answer: Quebec, Uniform, Alpha, India, Lima

10. KIND. Answer: Kilo, India, November, Delta

11. DEAF. Answer: Delta, Echo, Alpha, Foxtrot

12. MARS. Answer: Mike, Alpha, Romeo, Sierra

13. XEROX®. Answer: X-ray, Echo, Romeo, Oscar, X-ray

14. HAPPPY. Answer: Hotel, Alpha, Papa, Papa, Yankee

15. SIMPLE. Answer: Sierra, India, Mike, Papa, Lima, Echo

16. EXTRUDE. Answer: Echo, X-ray, Tango, Romeo, Uniform, Delta, Echo

17. FORTIFY. Answer: Foxtrot, Oscar, Romeo, Tango, India, Foxtrot, Yankee

18. ARMY. Answer: Alpha, Romeo, Mike, Yankee

19. NAVY. Answer: November, Alpha, Victor, Yankee

20. AIR FORCE. Answer: Alpha, India, Romeo, Foxtrot, Oscar, Romeo, Charlie, Echo

21. MARINES. Answer: Mike, Alpha, Romeo, India, November, Echo, Sierra

22. COAST GUARD. Answer: Charlie, Oscar, Alpha, Sierra, Tango, Golf, Uniform, Alpha, Romeo, Delta

23. CHEMICAL. Answer: Charlie, Hotel, Echo, Mike, India, Charlie, Alpha, Lima

24. OSTRICH. Answer: Oscar, Sierra, Tango, Romeo, India, Charlie, Hotel

25. HYDROGEN. Answer: Hotel, Yankee, Delta, Romeo, Oscar, Golf, Echo, November